I. INTRODUCTION

A. THE QUESTION AND THE THESIS

The Amazon region of South America spans over seven million square kilometers. While the majority of the region is located in present day Brazil, it can be found in nearly every country on the continent: Bolivia, Peru, Ecuador, Colombia, Venezuela, and Guyana. The Amazon's river and tributary system are responsible for depositing over one fifth of the fresh water which enters in the world's oceans.[1] In conjunction with the river, the Amazon is home to the world's largest tropical forest. Given that it did not pass through an ice age it has remained virtually unchanged for over 100,000,000 years. The Amazon region is responsible for the support of over one tenth of the known plant, animal, and insect species on earth.

Since Pedro Alvares Cabral discovered Brazil in 1500, the Amazon has been viewed by Brazil as a key to untold wealth and treasure. Thus, Brazilians have jealously guarded the Amazon region from foreign influences as they regard it as a means to achieve "*grandeza*".[2] Attempts to conquer the region

---

[1]Sue Branford and Oriel Glock, <u>The Last Frontier: Fighting over Land in the Amazon</u>, London: Zed Books, 1985, 8.

[2]<u>Grandeza</u> is the term coined by Brazilians to describe the superpower status that they believe Brazil is destined to attain. For a comprehensive discussion of this term see Jack Child, <u>Geopolitics of South America: Quarrels Among Neighbors</u>, New York: Praeger, 1985.

1

and extract this treasure have assumed both civilian and military forms, ranging from tax incentives for civilian development to direct military occupation of the frontier. The most recent attempt has been the <u>Calha Norte</u> (Northern Corridor) project.

The <u>Calha Norte</u> project consists of both military and civilian organizations which have established outposts along the northern borders in the states of Amazonas and Pará. The official goals of the project are geopolitical in nature in that they serve to demarcate the border, improve the local infrastructure, and promote economic development of the region.

The purpose of the thesis is to examine the rationale of the Brazilian Army in the <u>Calha Norte</u> project. Specifically, the paper proves that the rationale behind the 1993 project has expanded from the rationale of 1985. The paper further argues that this expanded rationale explains an increasing military presence in the Amazon.

With the conclusion of the Cold War, both civilian and military planners have searched for a new role for the Brazilian Armed Forces. Recent problems associated with the Amazon such as drug trafficking, gold mining, and environmental damage have caused the Brazilian Army to focus its attention on this region as a potential new role and mission. Additionally, the Army has been plagued by a shrinking budget due to Brazil's faltering economic performance.

My thesis argues that the rationale for Brazilian Army's involvement in the <u>Calha Norte</u> project has expanded from the original geopolitical motives to include justification for the military budget and restoration of the military institution's legitimacy.

B.   THESIS PURPOSE AND MAJOR RESEARCH QUESTIONS

The thesis analyzes the motivations behind the Brazilian Army and its expanding presence in the Amazon Basin. This analysis is important for the security interests of Brazil and its neighbors. If one reviews the major conflicts which have occurred within Latin America over the course of history, the evidence would show that a large percentage of these conflicts resulted from border disputes. Therefore, a buildup of Brazilian troops along a given border could be interpreted as threatening Brazil's regional neighbors. A second reason why this thesis is important relates to the interests of the United States in Brazil. The United States has specific regional concerns inside the Amazon, which include: promotion of regional democratization; increased efforts for combatting narco-trafficking; strengthening of civilian institutions; and an environmental concern for overdevelopment of the Amazon.[3]

As the United States progressively inserts itself into the role of international peacekeeper, understanding the rationale of these buildups can help it to mediate and resolve such disputes as they arise. The United States must recognize that Brazil is a significant power within South America and the

---

[3]For details on specific United States concerns see National Security Strategy of the United States, The White House, January 1993.

Third World. Consequently, Brazilian military motivations must be better understood by the U.S. policy makers so that they might work with the Brazil to realize U.S. regional goals and interests. This thesis provides an insight to these motivations through analysis of the Brazilian Army's project, <u>Calha Norte</u>. By focusing on the rationale for this program, the study uncovers the present day concerns of the Brazilian Army and uses them to explain its expanding roles and presence in the Amazon. The information is then used to examine the implications for U.S. security interests and policy options.

C.   METHODOLOGY AND ORGANIZATION OF THE THESIS

The case study methodology is employed by this study. The single case study of the <u>Calha Norte</u> project is analyzed over two periods in time: 1) <u>Calha Norte</u> as originated in 1985; and 2) the <u>Calha Norte</u> project today in 1993. The time periods were chosen to analyze the original rationale for the implementation of the <u>Calha Norte</u> project and the rationale for the expansion of the project. Within each case, the study will analyze the independent variables of geopolitical influences, military budget, and institutional legitimacy to prove the expanding rationale theory. Using this information, the paper will then assess the effect of these variables on the dependent variable of Army presence in the Amazon.

The thesis is divided into two distinct parts. The first provides a history for the development of Brazilian geopolitical thinking and an overview of the

4

<u>Calha Norte</u> project. It presents an evolution of the project and analyzes the findings in order to support the thesis of the project's changing rationale.

The second part examines the current regional situation and calculates the impact of Brazil's expanding military presence in the Amazon. It examines implications for U.S. security interests in the region with regard to U.S. stated interests, and suggests U.S. actions, vis-a-vis Brazil, to secure these interests.

The conclusion provides a summary of the pertinent findings and makes suggestions for further research.

II. HISTORICAL BRAZILIAN PRESENCE IN THE AMAZON

A. BRAZILIAN GEOPOLITICAL THINKING

The concept of geopolitical thinking originated in Germany with Friedrich

Ratzel (1844-1904). Ratzel suggested that the state had characteristics similar to

a living organism and that it should be studied from this perspective. His

framework of analysis posited that the state had to expand or die (to the

detriment or advantage of surrounding states). Additionally, he viewed

borders as "living frontiers" that were "dynamic and subject to change if the

stronger nations required expansion for their own existence."[4]

Rudolf Kjellen (Swedish, 1864-1922) added to Ratzel's ideas by proposing

that certain geographical factors added or detracted from a given state's

power. To Kjellen, the international stage pitted nations against one another in

a competition for the world's limited space and resources.[5] Later, Sir Halford

Mackinder (British, 1861-1947) added to the literature by suggesting that land

transport was the key to control and power. He argued that a nation could

---

[4]See Jack Child, <u>Geopolitics and Conflict in South America: Quarrels Among Neighbors</u>, New York: Praeger, 1985, 21.

[5]A more thorough presentation of Ratzel's and Kjellen's ideas are presented in Howard T. Pittman, "Geopolitics of the ABC Countries: a Comparison," Ph.D. dissertation, American University, 1981.

overcome obstacles, or enhance advantages, posed by geography through technology.[6]

Another German, Karl Haushofer (1869-1946), further developed the geopolitical concepts of expansion, conquest, and genocide. General Pinochet of Chile summarized Haushofer's concepts as follows:

- "*Lebensraum*, or the vital space that a state must have to breathe, grow, and expand.

- The notion that a state's frontiers must be natural and should expand out to the full extent of its *Lebensraum*.

- The concept of *autarky*, whereby the strong states develop their own complete economic base, including the defense economy, so that they will not be dependent on any other state.

- The idea that strong nation-states expand their spheres of influence out to an optimum maximum, which then becomes the pan-region associated with that state."[7]

These geopolitical concepts have been evident throughout the history of Brazil's development as a nation. The expansion of Portugal into the western regions of the Amazon (see below: **A History of Brazil in the Amazon**) were

---

[6]The technology that Mackinder was referring to was that of road building. For a better overview and comprehensive discussion of geopolitics see James E. Dougherty and Robert L. Pfaltzgraff, <u>Contending Theories of International Relations</u>, Philadelphia: J.B. Lippencott, 1971, 50-61.

[7]See Child, <u>Geopolitics and Conflict in South America: Quarrels Among Neighbors</u>, p.22. This summary was taken from Augusto Pinochet, <u>Geopolítica</u>, Santiago: Editorial Andrés Bello, 1974, 60-61.

illustrative of the strong influences of their geopolitical thinking. These values were subsequently passed on to the Brazilians as evidenced by their actions.

Brazilian geopolitical thinkers, led by Army officer Mario Travassos, differed from the German geopoliticians since they focused on concepts of "integral security and development."[8] In 1935, Travassos wrote that this needed to be accomplished by establishing "longitudinal Brazil". This concept encouraged Brazil to expand from its traditional coastal population towards the Amazon Heartland in order that Argentina's influence within the buffer states and the River Plate Basin be minimized.[9] According to Travassos, the establishment of this presence would give Brazil a much stronger base from which to project its power.

A second geopolitician which influenced Brazil's geopolitical policy is Everardo Backheuser. Backheuser promulgated the theory of "living frontiers," which posited that borders are fluid and flexible and respond to pressures which are exerted by the nations on each side. Backheuser argued that a strong nation would eventually expand into territories of weaker neighbors and therefore Brazil should strive to occupy its "empty spaces".

The most powerful proponent of Brazilian geopolitics in the latter half of the 20th century was General Golbery do Couto e Silva. General Golbery was

---

[8]See Child, 35.

[9]The buffer states consist of Uruguay, Paraguay, and Bolivia.

an official government advisor during most of the military regime (1964 to 1985). His writings and teachings were similar to that of Travassos and Backheuser in that they espoused national integration and effective use of national resources, effective occupation of internal territories, solidification of border areas, and economic development as vehicles to obtain *grandeza*.

Brazilian geopoliticians believe that order and discipline are essential ingredients for the nation to achieve international greatness.[10] Furthermore, national development greatly aids in the establishment of this order and discipline. The consequences of this type of thinking has been the promotion of several "themes" in Brazilian policy. The most prevalent theme, and the one most applicable to this discussion, is the Brazilian push to occupy "the empty spaces" of the Amazon basin.

The Brazilians view the Amazon as a place that houses untold mineral wealth necessary for economic independence. Additionally, they see the Amazon as a potential breeding ground for insurgencies since the government's presence and influence in the region is weak and disjointed.

---

[10]The concept of order in this case refers to both domestic and international security. Domestic order addresses internal subversions which would act to sway Brazil from its elite charted course towards grandeza. A good example of the concern for internal subversion would be the 1964 coup. For a good general overview see Gary W. Wynia, The Politics of Latin American Development, Third Edition, Cambridge: Cambridge University Press, 1990, 224-7. International order addresses the political stability of Brazil's bordering neighbors. An illustrative example of this can be found in the Suriname case study of Scott D. Tollefson, "Brazilian Arms Transfers, Ballistic Missiles, and Foreign Policy: The Search for Autonomy," Ph.D. dissertation, The Johns Hopkins University, 1991, 256-87.

Therefore, given Brazil's strong commitment to geopolitical principles it is not difficult to envision the aggressiveness with which Brazil has attempted to conquer the "empty spaces" of the Amazon. The following chapters will better highlight these geopolitical underpinnings of Brazilian policy and illustrate how it has been and continues to be a primary motivational factor for Brazilian presence in the Amazon.

B. HISTORY OF BRAZIL IN THE AMAZON

Prior to the Calha Norte project, Brazil's involvement in the Amazon region spanned three different regime types: (1) The Monarchy 1621-1889; (2) the Republic 1889-1964; and (3) the Military Regime 1964-1985. This section will look at each of these three regimes as well as their reasons for exploitation of the Amazon basin. Understanding the historical rationale and political thoughts of the past regimes are vital to understanding the current motivations of Brazil's Calha Norte project in settling the Amazon.

Each regime case study will focus on three separate factors: (1) political; (2) economic; and (3) geopolitical. Events or policies within a given case study will be classified as being political, economic, or geopolitical in nature. Classifications will be assigned giving consideration to a policy's stated purpose as well as the effect that it had on the region. For the purpose of this discussion a policy or event will be considered to be political in nature if it is intended to build political support or establish legitimacy for the regime in question. It will be considered economic if the policy is intended to enhance or expand the economic prosperity of the region. Finally, a policy will be considered geopolitical if the policy is designed to maintain or expand the country's power with respect to other regional countries.

1. The Monarchy, 1621-1889

a. *Political Analysis*

Given the nature of a monarchy and the definition of a political event, none of the government's policies were evaluated to have political overtones. Political benefit was neither sought nor gained during this time period.

b. *Economic Analysis*

Similar to the political analysis, the Portuguese crown did not use its policies to actively pursue an economic program to develop the Amazon region. However, this is not to say that economics were not a priority. Several policies during this time period clearly illustrate the desire of Portugal to enhance the economic prosperity of the Amazon region.

From the moment the Europeans discovered the Amazon, it was apparent that this region contained a plethora of natural wealth. It had been likened by some to the situations in the Orient and in black Africa which had already proved economically rewarding to many in Europe. The direct result of this comparison caused the European settlers to flood the Amazon and stake out their fortune in the forest.

The large influx of new settlers and the uniqueness of the region, prompted King Philip IV to create the states of Maranhão and Grão-Pará. They were to preside over the Amazon and deal directly with Portugal.[11] The settlers came to the Amazon with the intention of exploiting the abundant raw materials. To prevent an irreparable "strip mining" of the Amazon, the government responded by issuing explicit regulations that controlled not only the exploitation of the forest, but also the river basin as well.[12]

These regulations attempted to control the economic development of the region in two ways. First it specified quantities and time periods for extraction of the various Amazon natural resources. This is similar to the way modern countries control the same processes today. It served to allow for the extraction of the natural resources, yet prevented the unrestrained plundering of the forests. Secondly, the legislation gave tax incentives for the planting and replanting of certain vegetable wealth. This helped to restore certain plants in the region which were endangered due to

---

[11]See Branford and Glock, 10.

[12]For a comprehensive review of the specific economic policies of the monarchy see Arthur Cesar Ferreira Reis, "Economic History of the Brazilian Amazon", in <u>Man in the Amazon</u>, ed. by Charles Wagley, Gainesville, Florida: University Presses of Florida, 1974.

the indiscriminate exploitation. The ultimate goal of the legislative package

was aimed at providing for economic development of the region while

preventing colossal damage to the forests from unrestrained plundering.[13]

Probably the most significant economic event which influenced

government intervention in the region was the "rubber cycle". This was the

period of time which followed Charles Goodyear's discovery of the

vulcanization process for rubber in 1840. A combination of the increased

demand for rubber and its relative abundance in the Amazon region created

an economic flurry which has yet to be repeated.

During the 1900's at the height of this boom, the Amazona's

state income alone was over US$18 million. Rubber production and sales were

responsible for over 82 percent of this income. To protect this economic

windfall, the government stepped in to regulate the industry. Laws were

passed making it illegal for foreign interests to own the production or

transportation aspects of the rubber industry. In essence, this legislation

reserved all the rubber profits for the Brazilians and therefore strongly

encouraged further settlement and exploration of the region by the nationals.

However, international pressures quickly mounted against these unfair trading

---

[13]See Reis, p.35. It should also be noted that in addition to providing incentives in the region, Lisbon also provided incentives at home in Portugal to encourage the Amazonian economy. This was accomplished by prohibiting the sale of non-Pará items at home in the mother country. In effect they set up a monopoly for Amazonian products in the Portuguese market.

practices and the Portuguese crown was forced to rescind this legislation in 1857.[14]

c. Geopolitical Analysis

Throughout the reign of the monarchy, geopolitical concerns in the Amazon were continually demonstrated. During this time period numerous treaties were signed which revealed the importance of geopolitical thinking to the regime. An excellent example of these treaties would be the Treaty of Madrid (1750). This document has become a foundation for the evolution of geopolitics in South America.

The Treaty of Torsedillas was agreed upon by Spain and Portugal in 1494 and established the demarcation line illustrated in Figure 1. However, immediately following the treaty's approval Portugal began to push its settlements up the Amazon river basin. This was an attempt to occupy the entire watershed.[15] The Portuguese intent to occupy this land is best summed up by João the Fifth's decree: "You shall not only defend the lands which my vassals have discovered and occupied, but you will prevent the

---

[14]For a more in-depth discussion of the "rubber cycle" and its tremendous economic effects on the region see E. Bradford Burns, A History of Brazil (2nd edition), New York: Columbia University Press, 1980, 330-340.

[15]See p. 62 of Lewis A. Tambs, "Geopolitics of the Amazon", in Man in the Amazon, ed. by Charles Wagley, Gainesville, Florida: University of Florida Presses, 1973.

14

Spanish from advancing into our areas: moreover, you will promote

discoveries and possess all that you can, if not occupied by the Spanish."[16]

In 1750, when Portuguese occupation greatly exceeded their

legal titles to land tracts, Lisbon pushed for the ratification of the Treaty of

Madrid. The concept set forth the idea that actual possession of the land takes

precedence over simply having the title to the land. Their success in coercing

Spain to sign this treaty served as a prelude towards their acquisition of nearly

the entire Amazon region in a similar manner.

Another indication of the importance of the regime's geopolitical

thinking was the establishment of the Forte d'Óbidos. At d'Óbidos, the

Amazon river narrows to a single channel approximately 1800 meters wide

near the Atlantic mouth of the river. Control of this section effectively

determined who controlled the access to and from the river. This fort provides

the best example of what happened throughout the region; Portugal utilized

stone and mortar to keep in check any Castillian challenge to land claims in

the Amazon[17].

---

[16]See p. 22 of Marcos Carneiro de Mendonca, "Instrucões dadas pela rainha ao governados da capitania de Mato Grosso Dom Antonio Rolim de Moura em 19 de janeiro de 1749", *A Amazônia na era pombalina*, vol.1, Rio de Janeiro: Instituto Histórico e Geográfico Brasileiro. Translation Tambs, 67.

[17]For a much more thorough discussion of the fort system established by the Portuguese in the Amazon see Tambs, 63-6.

d. Period Evaluation

Although economics shaped Brazilian policy towards the Amazon during this period, it did not appear to be the dominant factor. The enacted legislation was weak and provided little direction for the country with regards to economic development of the region.[18] Additionally, those policies that incurred the criticism of the international community were changed relatively quickly with little protest from Lisbon. This may have been indicative of Portugal's commitment to fair trade practices, but more likely it was attributable to the fact that economic development was not the overriding concern of the regime.

On the other hand, geopolitical policy seemed to be taken much more seriously. Events of the time indicate that Portugal's driving force was to control and occupy the region. The extensive system of forts, unrestrained westward expansion to possess "all you can", and the numerous battles fought to claim, defend and reclaim territory all symbolize the monarchy's commitment towards achieving their geopolitical goals.

2.   The Republic 1889-1964

a. Political Analysis

Similar to the monarchy period, the government during the Republic (1889-1964) did not use the Amazon to achieve political ends. Thus

---

[18]See Reis, 35.

politics cannot be considered to have driven the government's policies with regards to development of the Amazon.

b. Economic Analysis

The major thrust of government involvement in the Amazon during this period stemmed from the rubber cycle just as it did during the monarchy. Monies from the rubber industry were used to transform Manaus and Belém into two of Brazil's most modern and beautiful cities, rivaling any contemporary European city.[19] Manaus became the first city in Brazil to have electric street lighting as well as numerous other amenities such as garbage collection, telephone service and efficient waterworks.[20] These services were instrumental in the governments effort towards encouraging Brazilians to settle and economically develop the Amazon. This is best illustrated by the population explosion of the Amazon at the turn of the century. In 1890 the population of the region was 380,000. By 1910 the population had grown to nearly 1,000,000. population explosion was experienced in the two cities of Manaus and Belém. This was directly attributable to the economic opportunities and quality of life that these two cities presented.

---

[19]Manaus and Belém served as the hub of rubber trade in the Amazon. These two cities were located on the Amazon river on opposite ends and marked the beginning and end of the rubber traders' route.

[20]For a more complete description of Manaus' and Belém's modernity see Burns, 335.

Once rubber was found to grow outside a "natural jungle" environment, rubber plantations spread throughout the Orient. This resulted in the Amazon losing its monopolistic position in the international rubber market. As the incentive to produce rubber in the region left, so too did the population. The Brazilian government was not able to prevent the economic and financial devastation which occurred in the region due to this exodus. An opportunity to reinvigorate the region occurred during the Second World War. To aid in resettling the region economically, Brazil negotiated the "Washington Accords" with the United States. These agreements provided Brazil the opportunity to supply the Allied war effort with rubber from the Amazon region.

In order to prevent a repeat of the previous mistakes which were made, Brazil set up several organizations to oversee and provide incentives to encourage the responsible development of the jungle. First, the government established the *Banco da Borracha* (Rubber Bank), which provided the financing necessary for rubber collection. This bank still exists today, but under a different name: Credit Bank of the Amazon Region. The expanded name is also indicative of the expanded responsibilities it has to finance not only rubber industries, but all industries in the region. Second was the creation of the *Serviço Especial de Saúde Pública* (Special Public Health Service). This organization was designed to assure health protection for the rubber gatherers, as their working conditions were less than ideal.[21] This agency was

critical in the government's efforts towards enticing workers back into the

region. Lastly the government created the Superintendency of the Amazon

Valley (SPVEA). SPVEA was charged with overall coordination of

development of the Amazon as well as promotion of investment and

responsible use of the land's resources.

c. Geopolitical Analysis

Brazil's application of geopolitics in the Amazon was unaffected

by the regime transition to a republic. The first illustration of this were the

events which surrounded the 1903 Brazilian and Bolivian Treaty of Petrópolis.

In 1878, the state of Ceará experienced a drought that caused over 54,000

Brazilians to migrate to Amazonia looking for relief and employment. With

this expanded labor pool from which to draw, the rubber industry pushed

further into the Amazon basin. This push eventually led into Bolivia's Alto

Acre, looking for additional sources of rubber. Although Bolivia had few

resources in the Acre region, it attempted to exercise its sovereignty over the

area. The Brazilian government was quick to respond with military force to

protect the Brazilian inhabitants and eventually established the Independent

---

[21]It should be noted that the life of a rubber gatherer was unusually harsh and
tedious. It consisted of long hours for relatively low pay and extremely poor working
conditions. The majority of the rubber gatherers were peasants who could be
compared to the migrant farm workers commonly found in the United States.

Republic of Acre in 1899. This territory was then officially annexed by Brazil through the Treaty of Petrópolis four years later.

Probably the most blatant display of Amazonian geopolitics was Kubitschek's construction of the new capital Brasília in the state of Goiás. Up until this time, Brazil's population was concentrated along the ocean and the riverbanks, which left the interior of the country essentially empty. Brasília represented the government's attempt to shift the nucleus of the country's population inward.

To fully understand the geopolitical underpinnings of this move towards the Amazon, one needs to recall the geopolitical history of Brazil as well as events which were developing at the time. Historically, over one half of Brazil's recognized territory was gained using the doctrine of *uti possidetis de facto* (possession takes precedence over legal title). Allowing a large portion of the Amazon frontier to remain unoccupied was analogous to providing an invitation for the bordering countries to reclaim their previously lost lands or possibly claim new ones. This Brazilian fear was certainly not unfounded as Peru had begun construction on the "Marginal Forest Highway". This expanded Peru's influence into the Andes Mountains and the Amazon region. In order to prevent Peru and other countries from occupying and therefore laying a legitimate claim to the territory, Brazil forcibly moved its population inland.[22] Thus Brasília, and all the construction associated with it, was to provide the "launching pad for the conquest of Amazonia."[23]

d. Period Evaluation

Economics seemingly played a large part in formulating Brazilian Amazon policy during this period. However, a critical review of these policies indicates that they were not the primary motivator of government intervention in the region. The policies that were intended to promote economic development during the rubber cycle achieved very little in that respect. They addressed the modernization and civilization problems of the region (see the Manaus and Belém examples) as well as distribution of profits, yet did nothing to address the efficiency of the rubber industry. Consequently when rubber was discovered to grow outside the region, the industry and the Amazon economy collapsed. The Rubber Defense Law of 1912 essentially encouraged the establishment of plantations (as in the Orient),

---

[22]The urgency with which Brazil viewed this problem is best illustrated by the breakneck speed with which Brasília was constructed. Begun in 1957, construction of the city continued for twenty-four hours per day, seven days a week, and fifty-two weeks a year. It was finally completed on April 21, 1960.

[23]This quote was taken from a speech given by a Brazilian official at the inauguration of Brasília. In addition to the construction of Brasília, this project consisted of over 11,000 miles of new roads connecting the new capital to the rest of the country. Exercising the *uti possidetis de facto* doctrine, these roads extended past Brazil's recognized borders into the Bolivian borderlands. See p. 137 Mauricio Vaitsman, *Brasília e Amazônia*, Rio de Janeiro: S.P.V.E.A., 1959. Translated and recorded by Tambs, 74.

but by this time Brazil had already lost the rubber market.[24] A government which had been concerned with economic modernization would have initially, instead of reactively, focused its policies on industrial efficacy and efficiency.

The insignificance of the regional economy on the government's agenda was again illustrated with the institutions set up during the post World War II era as noted above. These institutions were not only poorly funded, but they lacked the ability to enforce any rules which they enacted. As nothing was done to change this situation during the subsequent years, it provides another example of the low priority of economics.

Unlike economics, geopolitics received a good deal of attention and money with regards to the Amazon. The aggressive Brazilian occupation and subsequent annexation of the Bolivian territory (Treaty of Petrópolis) yield interesting insight as to the importance of geopolitics to the administration. This treaty, combined with the regime's unprecedented determination to complete the Brasília project and occupy the Amazon frontier, leaves no doubt that geopolitics again played a much more significant role than did economics.

3.   The Military Regime 1964-1985

a. *Political Analysis*

The first truly political overtures that were made with regards to developing the Amazon occurred in 1970 in response to a drought that

---

[24]See Burns, 339.

struck the Northeast region of Brazil. The drought, together with the already overcrowded living conditions of the Northeast, encouraged a situation that was ripe for social and political revolution.[25] To avoid political chaos, President Médici unveiled his plan for a National Integration Program (PIN) that would "open up the underpopulated Amazon Valley". The PIN was to have three main objectives: (1) the opening and integration of the Amazon by a new Transamazonian Highway; (2) the irrigation of 40,000 hectares in the Northeast; and (3) the creation of export corridors in the Northeast.[26]

In addition to solving a social crisis and securing the political situation in the Northeast, the PIN, more specifically the Highway, provided great symbolic and political value to the Government. It was an object that could be held before the Brazilian people as physical evidence that the government was making positive progress towards improving the conditions of the country. It procured the support of the important business constituency by doling out profitable construction contracts. Finally and most importantly, it diverted the nation's attention away from the oppression brought on by the regime.[27]

---

[25]See Branford and Glock, 60. As the focus of this paper is the Amazon, an in-depth discussion of the Northeastern situation is not presented here. For extensive discussion of this situation see Thomas Skidmore, The Politics of Military Rule, Oxford: Oxford University Press, 1988, 144-6.

[26]Ibid, 145.

[27]Ibid, 62.

b. Economic Analysis

The official government view of the Amazon during this period was best expressed by then under-secretary of the interior ministry, Raymundo Nonato de Castro's quote:

> The government's aim is economic occupation of the [Amazon], not its settlement. And this will be achieved through more technology and capital than labor.[28]

In addition to being used for political purposes, the Transamazonia Highway also served a stated purpose to aid in the economic maturation of the region. According to its designers, it was an "attempt to transfer rural populations to an environment and conditions propitious for their development into an economically productive sector."[29]

The government's desire to economically settle the region also resulted in the Amazon Development Plan. This plan was designed to promote high rates of economic growth while building up the country's productive forces. The government's expressed goal for the Amazon was for it to become economically integrated into the economy as quickly as possible in order to take advantage of it's potential. The first attempt by the government to accomplish this was to be coordinated through a SPVEA program. This

---

[28]See O Estado de São Paulo, 10 November, 1974.

[29]See Wenceslau Dyminski Wozniewicz, "The Amazonian Highway System", in Man in the Amazon, ed. by Charles Wagley, Gainesville, Florida: University of Florida Presses, 1973, 273.

program offered tax incentives and rebates to businessmen and corporations that were willing to set up and develop projects in the Amazon basin. This program was successful in that the government was able to attract over 350 projects to the region, which resulted in nearly $1 billion dollars in tax rebates over 10 years.[30]

A second program that the government used to economically integrate the basin was similar to the first "rebate scheme". It was comparable in that it offered federal monies for Amazon development, but it differed in that it was modified to be more of an industrial policy rather than one of the free market. This program, named Amazon Program of Farming (Polamazônia), consisted of 15 poles that targeted various industries for development.[31] Polamazônia offered cheap land in return for the promise that the owners would set up a specific "project" within five years of purchasing the properties. The project resulted in the government investment of nearly $300 million dollars over 3 years and the "settlement" of over 1,000,000 hectares of land.[32]

---

[30]See Branford and Glock, 44.

[31]See Branford and Glock, 73 for a more specific description of the various poles and their regional locations.

[32]The word "settlement" is used tenuously in that many of the corporations never set up the projects as required by the Polamazônia and defrauded the government of numerous tax credits. This topic will be further addressed in the evaluation portion of the paper.

c. Geopolitical Aspects

As with the other periods in Brazil, geopolitical maneuvering within the Amazon was evident during the military regime as well. Just as the Transamazon Highway served political and economic purposes, it also tried to alleviate the fears within the military officer corps that Brazil was on the verge of losing parts of the Amazon for want of settling it.[33] Compounding these fears was the discovery of extraordinary mineral wealth (specifically, iron ore), and the previously mentioned Peruvian construction of the "Marginal Forest Highway" that flanked the Eastern borders of the Amazon. The highway was then intended to provide the aforementioned political and economic benefits and establish the needed presence within the basin to prevent a *uti possidetis de facto* takeover.

In addition to the Highway, the military government took other steps to solidify its hold on the Amazon. These included the establishment of frontier military colonies at Príncipe de Beira, Tabatinga, Cucui, and Clevelandia do Norte; and the construction of *Rodovia Perimetral Norte* (Northern Perimeter Rim Road) that essentially served to "fence in" the Brazilian occupied territories of the Amazon.

Another move by the government that illustrated its geopolitical motivations was the establishment of the Executive Group for the Araguaia-

---

[33]See Skidmore, 146.

Tocatins Region (GETAT) by the National Security Council. This body was designed to oversee land distribution in the Amazon and was empowered "to overcome the bureaucratic limitations imposed on [the previous civilian organization] when it is dealing with land conflicts and issuing land titles."[34] These bureaucratic limitations concerned the requirement of INCRA (a civilian organization) to operate within the confines of the law. Unhindered by legal issues, the government now redistributed land from the peasant farmers to the wealthy businessmen and corporations. The redistribution was not for more efficient economic development, rather these businesses would establish a more militant and armed presence in the region in order to protect their investments. This redistribution of land therefore strengthened the Brazilian stronghold on the basin.

d. Period Analysis

This period saw the introduction of politics into Amazon policy making. While politics played an important role with regards to understanding a single facet of the Amazonian Highway, it can hardly be considered to be the primary motivator of government involvement in the Amazon.

Economics seemed to play an important role if one looks at the money the government invested in the economic programs of the period. But

---

[34]See Branford and Glock, 154.

looking beyond simply the financial aspect, evaluation of the programs administration would indicate otherwise. An example would be the initial economic investment program that focused on tax rebates and credits in exchange for private development of the Basin.

The agency in charge of the program was SPEVA and its charter required it to ensure that each proposed project was economically feasible. Additionally, after a project was approved, SPEVA was to verify that the project progressed as proposed and that the tax credits it received were reinvested in the region.[35] It was rare that either of these events occurred, which allowed for much of the government funds to be diverted to personal consumption by the corporations. In fact numerous people were employed by these corporations to assemble projects that looked good on paper, yet had no long term chance of viability. Their sole purpose was to obtain the tax rebates offered by the government.[36] Even more enlightening with regards to the government's priorities were the remarks of one official that "corruption was the price of development."[37]

The second development program was similar to the first in structure as well as problems. First, it concentrated its finances on programs that had no chance of succeeding even though the entrepreneurs may have

---

[35]See Branford and Glock, 45.

[36]Ibid, 50.

[37]Ibid, 45.

wanted to succeed. The best example of this was the cattle ranches that were promoted by the government's Polamazônia. Cattle ranching was an extremely inefficient operation because it cost more to grow the pasture grass which fed the cattle than the ranchers were able to get for the beef itself.[38] Second, it had similar problems in following up on the required progress of ranches that received government monies. A research team from the interior ministry found that almost two thirds of the ranches had not cleared and developed the land required by their proposals. Of the ranches that were operating, 90 percent of them were operating at 50 percent of capacity. Clearly these projects did not command the government's close attention and therefore cannot be considered to have been a priority at the time.

Geopolitics, as with the other periods of regime policymaking in the Amazon, was the primary concern of the military regime. Execution of the geopolitical initiatives was distinctly different from that of the economic programs. Unlike the lackadaisical supervisory approach of the economic enterprises, the geopolitical initiatives were recipients of close scrutiny from the government. This detailed attention ensured a timely completion regardless

---

[38]There are many good discussions available concerning the fragile ecosystem of the Amazon and its infertile soil. One of the more interesting accounts can be found by David Quammen, The Flight of the Iguana: A Sidelong View of Science and Nature, New York: Doubleday Press, 1988. This infertile soil makes it very expensive to raise beef as the costs for defoliants (necessary for weeds) and fertilizers normally exceed the prices obtained for the beef. For more on this discussion see Branford and Glock, 77-83.

of cost. It may even be argued that policies which were masqueraded as economic were in actuality geopolitical initiatives to guarantee that a strong presence was established and maintained in the Amazon. This could provide a plausible explanation as to why the government was so unconcerned with the progress of these enterprises.

4. Conclusions

Although economics and occasionally politics have been offered as interpretations for the motivations behind the Brazilian efforts to occupy the Amazon, these can provide only partial explanations of Brazil's push into Amazonia. <u>Regardless of regime type and economic situation, the geopolitical explanation is the only explanation that comprehensively describes Brazil's Amazon experience over the past 500 years</u>. This suggests that geopolitics in Brazil is not unique to a regime type, but rather it is a way of national thinking, shared by Brazil's leaders.

The previous discussion attempted to separate economics from geopolitics by way of a definition. This was done to highlight the point that the profit aspect of economics was not a primary motivator for Brazil's policies in the Amazon. However, it would be difficult to refute the point that economics play a large part in determining a country's power on the international stage. The best example of this would be the increasing importance and influence that Japan exerts on international affairs. Recalling that geopolitics was defined as enhancing a country's power with respect to its

31

competitors, it stands to reason that economics could fit into the framework of a geopolitical strategy.[39]

Several world events serve to highlight the importance of economics and geopolitics. First is the events which occurred within the Soviet Union during the 1980's through 1991. Previous policies that had emphasized the military aspect of geopolitical strategies while neglecting the economic aspects resulted in the eventual collapse of the state.

A second example illustrating the importance of economics and power would be the power and influence enjoyed by Saudi Arabia and other oil rich nations. With the exception of Iraq, the military component of these nations are insignificant in comparison to other national armies, yet most of them retain prominent positions in the world's political arena due to their economic clout.

A final example is the growing political strength of the "newly industrialized countries" (NICs) of the Pacific Rim. Their clout has dramatically increased to the point that the South Korean government intervened into domestic U.S. affairs and demanded restitution for Koreans whose property was damaged during the 1992 Los Angeles riots.

If we expand our economic definition to include not only the motives of profit but also the power associated with wealth, even more of

---

[39]See Daniel Papp, Contemporary International Relations: A Framework for Understanding(3rd Edition), New York: McMillan Publishing Co., 1991, 399-430.

Brazil's policies appear to support the geopolitical argument. This serves to reinforce the importance of geopolitics to Brazil's strategy in the Amazon regardless of regime type.

Understanding that geopolitical thinking has in the past been a primary motivator of Brazilian policy is extremely important for predicting and understanding future Brazilian policies and actions. The following section will introduce the <u>Calha Norte</u> project and detail its motivations as it was originally envisioned and then continue with looking at what motivates the project today.

III. THE <u>CALHA NORTE</u> PROJECT

A. <u>CALHA NORTE</u> 1985

1. Geographic Definition, Goals, and Project Structure

The <u>Calha Norte</u> project was established in 1985 as a joint venture by the Brazilian armed forces and the Brazilian ministries of Health, Education, Agrarian Reform, and Transportation to aid in the economic integration of the Amazon Basin into Brazil. The project concentrates on three central areas -- the frontier zone, the river region and the hinterlands.[40] Specific goals of the project are to:

- Increase bilateral relations with neighboring countries including trade;

- Eliminate drug trafficking in the region;

- Provide protection for the indigenous population;

- Restore and reinforce boundary demarcation;

- Promote regional development; and

- Increase military presence and security in the area.[41]

---

[40]See Susanna Hecht and Alexander Cockburn, <u>The Fate of the Forest: Developers, Destroyers, and Defenders of the Amazon,</u> New York: Verso Press, 1989, 119.

[41]See "The Role of the Brazilian Air Force in Amazonia Security and Development," USDAO document Brazil IR 6 809 00 58 89, enclosure (9), 15. See also Hecht and Cockburn, 119, and "Calha Norte", <u>Verde Oliva</u>, no. 118, March 1987, 4.

The project was designed to cover over 40 percent of the Brazilian Amazon region, comprising a total of 14 percent of all Brazilian territory. Specifically, Calha Norte encompasses a crooked corridor of land approximately 250 km wide and 6,500 km long for a total land area of 1,200,000 Km^2. The corridor is distributed within the states of Pará, Amazonas, and the territories of Amapá and Roraima. It's 6,500 km length travels the borders shared by Colombia, Venezuela, Guiana, Suriname, and French Guiana.[42] Figure 2 graphically depicts the geography of Calha Norte.

The project is physically located in the portion of the Amazon Forest that had been previously undeveloped. Access to the project even today is extremely limited by land vehicles as most roads are under construction or otherwise unreliable. During the rainy season, the project can be reached by river tributaries, but the majority of travel to and from the project is accomplished by air transport. The native population of the region consists of 51 small and ethnically diverse Indian cultures. However, an increasing number of migrants are drifting toward the region in search of gold and other mineral wealth. As of 1989, 537 mining claims had been filed with the Brazilian government, which represented nearly 20,000 goldminers.

---

[42]"Calha Norte," Verde Oliva, no. 118, March 1987, 3.

Historically, Brazil's armed forces have assumed the lead role with regard to nation building, and the Calha Norte project is no exception. The Army has assigned itself the mission of opening and securing the Amazon to be accomplished by a successful occupation of the region. Although the other services participate in Calha Norte, the Army provides the majority of support for the project.

The project proposes to establish a Brazilian presence along the border by creating eight outposts, manned by special frontier platoons. These outposts, headed by the Comando Militar da Amazonia (Amazon Military Command) located in Manaus, would serve the goals of border demarcation and regulation, as well as encouraging development. Each post would consist of approximately 70 soldiers, a food store, a school, a medical clinic, a community center, a Federal Police agency, a bank, an airport, and a system of communications.[43] The frontier posts are to serve as "city embryos," which will provide the foundations for future community development in the region.[44]

The extreme conditions experienced by the members of the Calha Norte project prompted the Army to create the *Centro de Instrução de Guerra na*

---

[43]See Lea Tarbutton, "The Calha Norte Project: Brazil's Armed Forces Modernization", *Armies of the World* (January - June 1991), 23.

[44]Ministerio do Exercito, Comando Militar da Amazonia, Seção de Planejamento. Paper presented during the Fifth Doctrinal Meeting between Brazil and the United States, Spring 1988, in Manaus, Brazil, translation Tarbutton.

Selva (CIGS -- Jungle Warfare Training Center), in Manaus, which would help individuals adapt to the jungle. The CIGS is to provide orientation seminars, physical and technical training, and psychological preparation for all Calha Norte personnel. To aid in this end, the project relies on recruiting from the local population to ease the necessary adjustment to the Amazon environment.

Additional logistical support for this project is provided by the 8th Military Region and the 12th Military Region, which are headquartered in Belém and Manaus respectively. The 8th Military Command operates two ocean-going vessels that are used to transport the heavy machinery and equipment required for platoon operations in the Amazon. The 12th Military Command provides tug and barge services as each frontier platoon is required to maintain its own riverine transportation for administrative and logistical support.[45]

The Brazilian Air Force and Navy also have interests in Calha Norte, but their roles are primarily supportive and logistical in nature. The Air Force has assumed the responsibility of building and maintaining the posts' airports in addition to providing the majority of transportation to and from the region. The Navy has been assigned the responsibility for security of the waterways. Additionally, the Navy has procured two hospital ships to

---

[45]See Tarbutton, 23.

render medical and dental services to the local Indians as well as the residents of the frontier posts.[46]

2. Analysis of Calha Norte 1985

Calha Norte was not the Brazilian armed forces' first attempt to extend their presence into the Amazon (see above: A History of Brazil in the Amazon). Events and ideas that had previously influenced the decision-making concerning this region continued to exert influence in 1985. This section analyzes these influences on the Calha Norte project from the perspectives of geopolitics, the military budget, and the legitimacy of the military as an institution.

For this discussion, geopolitical influences will be expanded from the previous definition to include any event that serves to affect the power relationship between two or more countries. With regards to the military budget category, an event will have significance if it influences the distribution of financial resources to the Armed Services. Lastly, the category of institutional legitimacy will analyze events that serve to affect either military or public perception of the Armed Forces role as defender of the Brazilian nation.

---

[46]LT Douglas R. Burnett, "Amazon Patrol", US Naval Proceedings, December 1978, 50-57.

a. Geopolitical Influences

For Brazil, as well as many other countries, issues of geopolitics have routinely been equated with issues associated with national security. The <u>Calha Norte</u> project is no exception. National security of the Amazon region was one the primary explanations offered justifying the 1985 project to the José Sarney Administration (1985-1990).[47] Of primary concern to the Brazilian strategists was infiltration of the Amazon by foreign forces, both governmental and nongovernmental. These forces included communist ideologies in Suriname, guerilla movements in Peru and Colombia, drug traffickers, and illegal miners. Former President Sarney vocalized this perception when he

said: I know today that we are ready to defend our borders that
are threatened today by drug traffic and by destabilizing
movements that employ violence in neighboring countries;
to protect our national resources from greed; to care for the
huge empty spaces willed to us by our ancestor.[48]

(1)   *Ideologies and Guerilla Movements.* Understanding the armed forces' sense of urgency related to implementing <u>Calha Norte</u> is best explained by reviewing the major events that preceded the project's announcement. To the Brazilian elite, the most pressing issues that threatened the Amazon were the various destabilizing political situations surrounding

---

[47]See "Government to Implement 'Calha Norte' Project", <u>Folha De Sao Paulo</u>, 31 October 1986, 6.

[48]See José Sarney, "Transição é Feita Com as Forças Armadas", <u>O Estado de São Paulo</u>, 18 December 1987.

Brazil during the early 1980's in Suriname, Colombia, and Peru. The instability in Suriname resulted from Cuban guerrillas sent by Castro to shore up the Bouterse regime. Lieutenant Colonel Desire Bouterse came to power during a February 1980 coup against a freely-elected Surinamese government. Bouterse was responsible for installing leftist dictatorship, which established closer ties to the Soviet Union and Cuba. Like the Soviet Union and Cuba, Bouterse was highly intolerant of political opposition, which led him to order the execution of 15 prominent opposition leaders in 1982.[49] The direct result of these executions was the suspension of Western trade and economic aid, leaving Suriname in a very difficult economic condition.

As Bouterse had strengthened ties to Cuba following his assumption of power, Cuba was quick to fill this void left by the Western nations. By the end of 1982, Cuba was supplying Suriname with between 30 and 100 "advisors" as well as training for Surinamese commandos and presidential bodyguards.[50]

The Brazilian military regime had assumed power to fend off communist advances inside Brazil. It was not surprising then that they

---

[49]See Celestine Bohlen, "OAS Criticizes Suriname Over Human Rights," Washington Post, 13 October 1983.

[50]For a more in depth discussion of the Surinamese situation and the resultant Brazilian response see Scott D. Tollefson, "Brazilian Arms Transfers, Ballistic Missiles, and Foreign Policy: The Search for Autonomy," Ph.D. dissertation, The Johns Hopkins University, 1991.

perceived Cuba's expanding influence in Suriname as a threat to their own political stability.[51] The Brazilian response took on two facets to combat the situation in Suriname. The first facet was "offensive" in nature in that Brazil sent a delegation to Suriname to offer Brazilian forces and resources to replace those that Cuba had sent. The implication was that if this offer was refused, military action against Suriname would result.[52]

The second facet of the response was "defensive" in nature, in that Brazil took measures to strengthen their borders against the infiltration of Marxist ideology. The Surinamese situation was probably the single biggest catalyst for the Calha Norte project as it spurred the army to invest US$80 million for the border strengthening. This argument was used to provide the foundation for the military's rationale to institute the Calha Norte project. The feeling within the military was that such an ideological infiltration into Brazil was a direct assault on the nation's sovereignty.[53] The situations in Peru and Colombia presented a similar affront to Brazilian sovereignty. In Peru, the Sendero Luminoso (Shining Path) represented a serious threat not only to the

---

[51]See "Army Concerned over Cubans In Suriname," Folha de São Paulo, in Portuguese, 3 April 1983, 9, translated by FBIS, 7 April 1983. See also "Army to Army Relationships: Past-Present-Future", Brazilian Military brief presented to the U.S. Army Policy Council, 6 May 1986, by Colonel Sam A. Gray, U.S. Army Attaché Brazil.

[52]See Tollefson, 264-267.

[53]U.S. Government Official, interview by author, Washington D.C., March 31 1993. See also "Northern Borders Being Strengthened: Army Concerned over Spread of Marxist Influence," Latin America Regional Reports: Brazil, RB-87-01, 1 January 1986, 3.

Peruvian government, but also to Brazil. The Shining Path, a Maoist and Marxist revolutionary movement within Peru, is committed to overthrowing the current government through violent insurrection. Its goal, consistent with Maoist tenets, is to mobilize the rural peasant masses alongside the urban shantytown dwellers to rise up against the central government. Using the "proletariat" masses located outside the cities, Sendero's leadership is attempting to squeeze the cities and government into submission.[54]

The movement primarily operates in the Andean highlands and focuses on being the first "continuing and positive outside contact for many peasants."[55] David Scott Palmer, an expert on the Shining Path, has noted, "the greatest contact between the peasantry and Sendero tended to be those of least contact between the peasantry and the government." Examples of regions where the government maintains minimal involvement and subsequently where Sendero flourishes, are reported in the 1981 Ayacucho department census. For a population of 500,000 people, Ayacucho boasted 30 doctors, 366 hospital beds, 827 telephones, and 44 kilometers of paved road.[56]

---

[54]See Gordon H. McCormick, "From the Sierra to the Cities: The Urban Campaign of the Shining Path," RAND, R-4150-USDP, 1992, 7. For a more detailed discussion of the tactics and ideologies of the Shining Path see also David Scott Palmer, editor, The Shining Path of Peru, New York: St. Martin's Press, 1992, and Gordon H. McCormick, "The Shining Path and the Future of Peru," RAND, R-3781-DOS/OSD, March 1990.

[55]See David Scott Palmer, "Rebellion in Rural Peru: The Origins and Evolutions of Sendero Luminoso," *Comparative Politics*, volume 17, January 1986, 137.

[56]Ibid, 137.

This information was instrumental in the formulation and defense of the Calha Norte project.[57] The Brazilian military feared that clashes between Peruvian federal troops and the Sendero Luminoso could cause the revolutionaries to seek a safe haven inside an uncontrolled Brazilian Amazon.[58] If Sendero were to establish strongholds in the Amazon, not only would it be an affront to Brazil's sovereignty in the region, but it could lead to the expansion of the movement into the Brazilian political arena.

The Calha Norte project was designed not only to establish the military presence in the region, which would deter the Shining Path from settling in Brazil, but also at taking away potential bases of support. Peru's approach to eradicating Sendero had been an exclusively military approach, which by most evaluations had failed. Even the recent capture of leader Guzman has not deterred the group from continuing with their strategy of mobilizing peasant masses. Brazil's Calha Norte project differed from the Peruvian approach in that it did not use the military to keep the guerilla movement in check, rather it provided positive and continuing government contact with the local residents. The latter part was accomplished by the

---

[57]See "Army to Army Relationships: Past-Present-Future," brief presented to the U.S. Army Policy Council, 6 May 1986, by Colonel Sam A. Gray, USA Attache, Brazil.

[58]See Andrew Hurrell, "The Politics of Amazonian Deforestation," The Journal of Latin American Studies, volume 23, February 1991, 206.

frontier post schools, hospitals, and dental clinics that made up the frontier post community.[59]

In addition to the Shining Path in Peru, the M-19 organization in Colombia also provided the stimulus for the Calha Norte project. The M-19 is a faction of the Colombian guerilla group FARC. Like the FARC, the M-19 is dedicated to the overthrow of the Colombian government using violent means as necessary. Although this organization does not share the ideological tenets of the Shining Path, they are still a source of instability along the Brazilian Amazon Border.[60]

In 1985, the M-19 concerned the Brazilian military for two reasons: illegal mining operations in the Amazon as well as the unauthorized use of Brazilian territories to establish bases of operations. A 1985 newspaper report indicated that the M-19 had set up camps along the Negro River in the Amazon near the Mapapi and Panapana gold fields.[61] These reports indicated that the M-19 was using the Brazilian Amazon as a safe haven to evade the Colombian authorities. Furthermore, they were using the local

---

[59]Calha Norte, Brazilian Military pamphlet, 1987, 3. This pamphlet identifies specific goals of improving the social services and infrastructure available to the Brazilian Indians.

[60]"Army Carries Out Maneuvers Near Colombian Border," Folha de São Paulo, in Portuguese, 11 December 1985, 1, translated in FBIS, volume VI, 13 December 1985, D5.

[61]"Army Investigating M-19 Border Operations," O Estado de São Paulo, in Portuguese, 21 December 1985, 5, translated in FBIS, volume VI, 26 December 1985, D4.

Indian population to search for gold as a means of financing their guerilla activities inside Colombia.

(2)   *Drug Trafficking.* The increased amount of drug trafficking in the Amazon region has provided additional impetus for the implementation of the <u>Calha Norte</u> project. A report released in 1991 indicated that 60% of the cocaine arriving in Europe passed through Brazil.[62] The increased attention that smugglers and producers have been receiving from the governments of Peru and Colombia have resulted in a large number of these organizations relocating to the Brazilian Amazon, where there has been little government presence.[63] Furthermore, Brazil is a major producer of coca-manufacturing chemicals such as ether, acetone and benzine. Brazil will only sell these chemicals to legitimate businesses. Therefore, traffickers have found it beneficial to locate their labs in Brazil where they can avoid the scrutinization of Brazilian customs. This makes it much easier to acquire these chemicals. By 1988, Brazil was noted to be a major player in the international narcotics

---

[62]Don Bohning, "Suriname Emerges as Shipping Point for Europe's Drugs," <u>Miami Herald</u>, 23 June 1991, 15A. See also "Police Uncover 'New' Medellin Cartel Drug Route," <u>Brasilia Radio Nacional de Amazonia</u>, in Portuguese, 29 November 1989, translated in <u>FBIS</u>, 30 November 1989, 44-45.

[63]Jesus E. Brando, "Narcotrafico tomo como base el Caribe: Oriente se ha convertido en puente de sangre y coca [Drug Trafficking Took Caribbean as Base: The East has Become a Bridge of Blood and Cocaine]," <u>Nacional</u>, in Spanish, 23 July 1991, translated in <u>InfoSouth</u>, accession no. 49708.

chain, participating in all facets of the trade.[64] Brazilian Army officials and

other strategists have indicated they view drug trafficking to be a major issue

of national security with a potential of transforming the Amazon into another

Vietnam.[65]

The Calha Norte project provided the Brazilian military

response to this increased trafficking.[66] Normally the drug operations were

tracked and prosecuted by the Brazilian Federal Police (PF) given that the

Army is prevented by the Brazilian Constitution from participating in law

enforcement activities. Consequently, the project was not designed to

apprehend illegal traffickers, it merely deterred them from crossing the border

and establishing a presence in the Amazon.[67] In fact, the 5th Special Frontier

Battalion was set up and specifically located in São Gabriel da Cachoeira with

---

[64]Alan Riding, "Brazil Now a Vital Crossroad for Latin Cocaine Traffickers," The New York Times, 28 August 1988, section 1.1.

[65]Anonymous, "Na Amazonia, o desafio [In the Amazon, the Challenge]," Estado de Sao Paulo, in Portuguese, 7 September 1989, translated by InfoSouth, accession no. 19194. The author of this article expressed fears that an increasing drug economy in the Amazon would lead to unwanted international attention, specifically from the United States. Brazil feared that as the Amazon became a major production and transhipment route for cocaine, US advisors would be forced upon them, creating a situation similar to Vietnam.

[66]Andrew Hurrell, "The Politics of Amazonian Deforestation," The Journal of Latin American Studies, volume 23, February 1991, 206.

[67]"Military to Strengthen Border Against Traffickers," Madrid EFE, in Spanish, 30 March 1987, translated in FBIS, 2 April 1987, D2. See also "Army Ministry Investments in 1987 Modernization Surveyed," Folha de São Paulo, in Portuguese, 10 January 1988, translated in JPRS, LAM-88-009, 3 March 1988, 10-11.

Battalion was set up and specifically located in São Gabriel da Cachoeira with this mission in mind. These daily operations of the frontier posts confirm this design, in that frontier soldiers do not actively search for drug trafficking operations. If operations are encountered, the traffickers are apprehended and turned over to the PF members stationed at the frontier posts, who in turn prosecute the perpetrators.[68]

(3) *Wildcat (illegal) Mining Operations.* Lastly, support for the Calha Norte project was boosted in 1985 by the illegal mining of Amazonian gold and mineral wealth.[69] The military viewed the Amazon's illegal mine operations as the stealing of national assets. A study performed by the National Department of Mineral Production (DNPM) estimates that between 1977 and 1986, 1,569 tons of gold were lost due to smuggling operations, compared to the 167 tons that were recovered through legitimate mining methods. Brazil estimated these losses to have cost them US$22.6 billion, which was equivalent to nearly 20 percent of the external national debt.[70] Based on the results of this study, the DNPM called for greater government

---

[68]U.S. government official, interview by author, Quantico, VA, 30 April 1993.

[69]A study performed by the Hudson Institute demonstrated that there are US$1.7 trillion worth of mineral reserves in the Amazon region. See "Amazon Commander Scores Industrialized Nations," O Globo, in Portuguese, 19 July 1991, 7, translated and reported in FBIS, LAT-91-141, 23 July 1991, 18.

[70]"Revenue Losses From Wildcat Gold Prospecting Assessed," Correiro Braziliense, in Portuguese, 14 February 1988, translated in IPRS, LAM-88-015, 15 April 1988, 19-20.

the regions containing prospecting operations to stem the massive outflow of capitol.[71]

In addition to the financial losses incurred as a result of the prospecting, Brazilian military officials also viewed the problem as a loss of sovereignty issue. This was because the borders were frequently transversed illegally by Colombian and Venezuelan nationals to work in these wildcat mines. Similar to the drug trafficking issue, the military wanted to establish a presence in the Amazon that would deter further exploitation of these national resources as well as strengthen the borders.[72]

b. Budgetary Influences

Funding and other financial concerns played small inconsequential parts with regards to the rationale of the Calha Norte project. This was clearly evident from the funding the military received as well as ease which they obtained these resources. Although the military had just recently retired from power in 1985, they were far from powerless with regards to influencing civilian administrative policies. In fact, prior to retiring, the Army generals skillfully maneuvered themselves into political positions within the

---

[71]Ibid, 20.

[72]"Army Ministry Investments in 1987 Modernization Surveyed," Folha de São Paulo, in Portuguese, 10 January 1988, translated in JPRS, LAM-88-009, 3 March 1988, 10-11.

government so as to be able to control and reinforce corporate military goals.[73] One of the more illustrative examples of this was the control they exerted over the National Service for Intelligence (SNI) and its successor agencies. Their control of the national intelligence and information network allowed them to exert significant influence in all aspects of the new administration.

Examples of this influence can be found with the initial and subsequent funding of the Calha Norte project. Even though Brazil was experiencing an economic crisis in 1986, the Army still received generous authorizations for its programs. With little hesitation, Congress appropriated in 1985 an initial US$180 million and US$250 million for each subsequent year, to support of the *Força Terreste 90* (FT-90), the armed forces' modernization program that included the Calha Norte project.[74] More interesting than the appropriation is the fact that the government had little idea as to where it would obtain the monies to fund this program. Some reports indicated that

[73]Daniel Zirker, "The Civil-Military Mediators in Post-1985 Brazil," Journal of Political and Military Sociology, vol. 19, 1991, 48-49. See also Ken Conca, "Technology, The Military, and Democracy in Brazil," Journal of Interamerican Studies and World Affairs, Spring 1992, 150-1.

[74]"Army Modernization is Under Way," Latin America Regional Reports: Brazil, RB-86-03, 14 March 1986, 5. See also "Armed Forces to Get US$250m a Year: Modernization of Weaponry and Communications Systems," Latin American Regional Reports: Brazil, RB-86-07, 14 August 1986, 5.

the money was to be transferred from the budgets of other agencies, such as the ministries of communications, health, and interior.[75]

At the conclusion of 1987, the Army had used up its allotted appropriations for the FT-90 project. In order to continue with the project, the Army lobbied Congress and successfully gained the authorization for an additional Cz$4.7 billion (approximately US$350 million at the time). This new amount alone was equivalent to 1.2 percent of the government deficit forecast for 1987.[76] The influence and power that the military enjoyed during this period enabled them to forward this request to the Congress with little justification for its spending. In fact, not only did the Army continue to ask for more money, but a statement by the armed forces constitutional commission additionally proposed that "no [monetary] limits should be established in the defense budgets."[77] Much of this autonomy the military had with regard to its budget stemmed from the perception within Brazil that the financial investment in the military would lead to a higher "professionalization". This increased professionalization would inhibit the armed forces from political interventions, as in the coup of 1964.[78]

---

[75]Ibid, 5.

[76]"Purchases, Costs of Army FT-90 Modernization Project Viewed," O Estado de São Paulo, in Portuguese, 18 September 1987, 18, translated by IPRS.

[77]"Military Wants Emergency Measures in Constitution," O Globo, in Portuguese, 22 February 1986, 3, translated by FBIS, volume VI, 27 February 1986, D1.

[78]Ibid, 18.

c. *Institutional Legitimacy Influences*

The 1964 Brazilian Army enjoyed a degree of institutional legitimacy from the general populace. This was most evident during the military's 1964 coup of the João Goulart government, when President Goulart's request for Brazilians to "rush the barricades" in protest of the coup was answered with a loud silence.[79] In fact, not only did the coup go unprotested by most Brazilians, but it was cheered and regarded as the "greatest day in [Brazilian] history."[80]

In 1985, even though the military government had stepped down due to being discredited with 21 years of political rule, the military as institution retained substantial legitimacy. Therefore, just as budgetary politics had little to no influence concerning the rationale for Calha Norte, the same was true for questions of institutional legitimacy or the *raison d'etre* for the military and its function.

During the period between 1985 and 1987, the military had successfully defended, and the public accepted, their role and mission within Brazilian society as guarantor of the national security both externally and internally. Efforts by civilian officials to restrict the military institution with

---

[79]Burns, 502-3.

[80]Octavio Ianni, Crisis in Brazil, translated by Phyllis B. Eveleth, New York: Columbia University Press, 1970, 128.

regards to Constitutional responsibilities failed, as did their efforts to combine the services under a unified Ministry of Defense.[81]

Following the resignation from power by the Armed forces in 1985, a movement was initiated to scale down the institutional military's responsibilities within Brazilian society. A draft constitution approved in 1986 by the Constitutional Studies Provisional Commission, articulated the Armed Forces' responsibility to include only external defense of the country.[82] The immediate response from the military was a reiteration of their historical constitutional mission of both internal and external defense. Army Minister General Leonidas Pires Goncalves was quoted as saying "[internal defense] is our constitutional mission, and we will not give it up now or in the future."[83] Meetings held by the Army's officials to discuss the new constitutional draft did not even include debate over the proposed new role for the armed forces institution, because they did not consider reduced responsibilities a legitimate option. The position by the Army, retaining both external and internal defense

[81]Ken Conca, "Technology, The Military, and Democracy in Brazil," Journal of Interamerican Studies and World Affairs, Spring 1992, 150-1.

[82]"Military Ministers Reject Reductions of Duties," O Estado de Sao Paulo, in Portuguese, 10 June 1986, 1, translated in FBIS, volume VI, 17 June 1986, D2.

[83]"Armed Forces Concerned Over New Military Role," O Estado de Sao Paulo, in Portuguese, 7 June 1986, 4, translated in FBIS, volume VI, 13 June 1986, D1.

responsibilities for the armed forces, was eventually upheld in the 1988 constitution.[84]

In addition to the responsibilities issue, a second debate was held to attempt to unite the three services under one ministry of defense, thereby reducing the powers of each of the individual service institutions. This effort was also derailed by the armed forces.[85]

B. CALHA NORTE 1993

1. Geographic Definition, Goals, and Project Structure

The geographical definition of the Calha Norte project has not changed in its scope in that it still focuses on an area of land approximately 1,200,000 km^2 encompassing the frontier lands, the river regions, and the hinterlands of the Amazon. What has changed, however, has been the structure of the project as well as the stated goals of the project. While command structure has remained the same the number of posts has increased from eight to nineteen.[86] These posts fall under the five Special Frontier Battalions as follows:

---

[84]"Armed Forces Role," Folha de Sao Paulo, in Portuguese, 27 August 1988, A-5, translated in FBIS, LAT-88-167, 29 August 1988, 37.

[85]Conca, 148.

[86]"Implementation of Calha Norte Project Urged," Correiro Braziliense, in Portuguese, 16 November 1990, 5, translated in FBIS, LAT-91-006, 9 January 1991, 24.

- First Special Frontier Battalion headquartered in Tabatinga with Special Frontier Platoons in Vila Bittencourt and Ipiranga.

- Second Special Frontier Battalion headquartered in Boa Vista with Special Frontier Platoons in Surucucu, Auaris, Erico, BV-8, Normandia, and Bonfim.

- Third Special Frontier Battalion headquartered in Macapá, with Special Frontier Platoons in Oiapoque and Tirios.

- Fourth Special Frontier Battalion headquartered in Rio Branco.

- Fifth Special Frontier Battalion headquartered in São Gabriel da Cachoeira with Special Frontier Platoons in Iauarete, Querari, São Joaquim, Maturaca, and Cucui.

In addition to the increased posts, additional support battalions have moved or are planned to move into the Amazon region in support of the Calha Norte project. Specifically, the 17th Motorized Infantry Battalion is to be transferred from Cruz Alta to become the 17th Jungle Infantry Battalion. The 61st Motorized Infantry Battalion in Santo Angelo will be restationed as the 61st Jungle Infantry Battalion. Lastly the 16th Engineering and Construction Battalion at Cruzeiro do Sul will be relocated to Rio Branco. Furthermore, the Army outlined plans to open two additional garrisons at Tunui and Asunção do Icana in the Rio Negro region, known as Dog Head.[87]

Furthermore, the goals have changed slightly from the original six goals published in 1986 (see Calha Norte 1985: Geographic Definition, Goals, and Structure above). All the stated goals remained the same, with the

---

[87]"Calha Norte Project Given Higher Priority," Jornal do Brasil, in Portuguese, 2 November 1992, 4, translated in FBIS, LAT-92-243, 17 December 1992, 26-7.

exception of the drug trafficking mission, which was replaced by a commitment to improve social services.[88] While improved social services had been a consequence of the Army's occupation of the Amazon, it had not previously been a stated goal.

2. Analysis of Calha Norte 1993

This section will analyze the Calha Norte project using the same independent variables of 1985 section: geopolitics, military budget, and institutional legitimacy. The definitions for each of these variables will be identical to the ones used in the 1985 section.

a. Geopolitical Influences

Similar to the rationale involved with the Calha Norte project in 1985, geopolitics still has great influence with regard to the Army's desire to occupy the Amazon. The same factors that shape the geopolitical agenda in 1993 have changed slightly, but for the most part are the same as they were in 1985. Regional guerrilla operations, drug trafficking, and wildcat mining operations have worked together to make the implementation of Calha Norte of premier importance to the Army.

---

[88]Boletim Informativo, No. 26, XX Conferêcia Dos Exércitos Americanos 1992/1993, August 1992, 26. Although a counterdrug mission is no longer specifically designated as a mission for the Calha Norte project, it still remains a high priority for the military. An expanded discussion of this issue occurs later in this chapter.

(1)   *Ideologies and Regional Guerrilla Operations.* The extent and location of these threats is probably the area which has changed most significantly over the last eight years. In 1985 the concerns were focused on communism infiltrating Brazil from Suriname, and political guerrilla activity from Peru and Colombia. Since then, some of these threats have subsided such as the communist threat from Suriname. With the demise of the Soviet Union, communist expansionism is no longer a viable threat to the international community, even from Cuba, which is experiencing its own difficulties. In fact, not only does Cuba no longer provide a threat to Brazil, but Brazil is courting Cuba as a potential market for Brazilian goods.[89]

Although the threat of communism has dissipated, it has been replaced by a military fear of foreign government internationalization of the Amazon region for economic purposes. This fear first surfaced in 1989 when the Executive Intelligence Review, a Lyndon LaRouche publication, reported a U.S. interest in invading the Amazon similar to other Latin American campaigns in Panama and Grenada.[90] Complicating the situation, United Nations officials then verbalized potential plans to transfer excess Asian

---

[89]"Franco Meets With Cuban Envoy, Considers Visit to Cuba," O Estado São Paulo, in Portuguese, 25 March 1993, 6, translated in FBIS, LAT-93-058, 29 March 1993, 30. See also "Implementation of Air Agreement With Cuba Announced," Jornal do Brasil, in Portuguese, 26 February 1993, 2, translated in FBIS, LAT-93-044, 9 March 1993, 6.

[90]U.S. Government official, Department of State, interviewed by author, 1 April 1993.

populations to the Amazon region and advanced the notion that Brazil be recognized as having only 'relative sovereignty' over the Amazon.[91] The accuracy of the LaRouche report was highly questionable. Nonetheless, both these reports served to incite the chief of the Military Command of the Amazon (CMA), General Antenor de Santa Cruz Abreu, to respond with vows to "transform the Amazon into a new Vietnam" for the industrialized countries.[92]

The majority of Brazilians do not believe that there is a true international threat to the Amazon, illustrated by (former environmental secretary) José Lutzenburger's dismissal of the idea as "ridiculous nonsense". Even within military circles the idea is not widely held as a general truth. One U.S. government official in Brazil estimated that less than 1 percent of the military take this claim seriously.[93] He hastened to add however, that this is a formidable 1 percent. This was illustrated by the official statements made on behalf of the Calha Norte project. Army Minister Zenildo Zoroastro de Lucena

---

[91]"'Internationalisation' of Amazonia Rallying-Point for Military Hardliners," Latin America Regional Reports: Brazil, RB-92-03, 19 March 1992, 1.

[92]General to Fight Internationalization of Amazon," Folha de São Paulo, in Portuguese, 23 July 1991, 1, translated in FBIS, LAT-91-147, 24.

[93]U.S. government official, Brasilia, phone interview by author, 17 May 1993.

defended increasing the resources associated with the project until the "internationalization theories" could be thoroughly evaluated.[94]

The instabilities due to guerrilla operations along the border have changed as well. The supposed threat that the military perceived from the Shining Path has not materialized either. However, the threat from the M-19 guerrilla organization has exceeded all the military's expectations. Their operations have resulted in frequent violations of the border between Colombia and Brazil, but more importantly have taken the lives of Brazilian soldiers stationed in the border regions. In February 1991, Colombian guerrillas attacked and killed three Brazilian soldiers and wounded nine others in an attempt to free a group of miners that the military had apprehended.[95] This event immediately sparked a cry from the military as well as the general population for an increased presence in this region. The result was an additional Cz$300 million of funding for the Calha Norte project and the creation of a special platoon along the Rio Traira where the incident took place.[96]

---

[94]"Calha Norte Project Given Higher Priority," Jornal do Brasil, in Portuguese, 2 November 1992, 4, translated in FBIS, LAT-92-243, 17 December 1992, 26.

[95]"Brazilian Border Operations Draw Attention," El Tiempo, in Spanish, 26 March 1991, 6A, translated by FBIS, LAT-91-062, 1 April 1991, 37.

[96]"Calha Norte Project Given Higher Priority," Jornal do Brasil, in Portuguese, 2 November 1992, 4, translated in FBIS, LAT-92-243, 17 December 1992, 26-27.

(2) *Drug Trafficking.* Drug trafficking has continued to make inroads into Brazil, making it a principal drug trafficking route for transport of South American cocaine to the United States and Europe.[97] Although it remains a problem within Brazil, it has apparently been dropped from the rationale of Calha Norte project. In 1985, the area known as Dog Head, was organized with its main goal as combatting the drug trafficking in the region and this goal was specifically listed in the Army's stated objectives for the project. In a 1993 information bulletin published by the Brazilian Army, Calha Norte's goals failed to address the issue of drug trafficking. However, this does not come as a surprise. For years the Brazilian military has resisted U.S. pressure to accept a role in the counterdrug campaign. Their reasons for hesitancy include a lack of training for the mission, Constitutional prohibition, and opportunities for corruption.[98]

The dropping of the counterdrug goal from the project's objectives could be misleading with regards to the rationale of the project itself. It would seem that this is no longer a concern of the military especially when the former CMA, General Santa Cruz, made statements to the press that

---

[97]"Drug Trafficking Rise Blamed on Police Crisis," EFE (Madrid), in Spanish, 19 February 1993, translated in FBIS, LAT-93-034, 23 February 1993, 22.

[98]Roy I. Kitchener, "The Brazilian Military: Its Role in Counter-Drug Activities," Masters Thesis, Naval Postgraduate School, Monterey California, June 1992. This thesis addresses both stated and unstated reasons for the military's hesitancy to become involved in the drug campaign.

indicated he thought the problem of drugs coming into the Amazon was "a lot of crap." However, this view is countered by a 1990 report which emphasized the problems caused by narcotics traffic in the region and went further to recommend rapid implementation of the Calha Norte project as a means of responding to these problems.[99]

Probably the best explanation for the removal of narco-trafficking as a goal of the project lies within the project structure. In 1985, the Calha Norte project was started as a joint venture between several civilian and military ministries. As the project progressed, the civilian ministries began to pull out due to inadequate funding and inability to attract personnel to work in the jungle regions.[100] Because of this, the military was forced to take on a much greater role than the plan had initially stipulated. Instead of supplying simply a military presence to the region, the Army officers became the doctors, the schoolteachers, the law enforcers and the legal system of the project's settlements. Given that the Calha Norte had in essence become a military

---

[99]"Implementation of Calha Norte Project Urged," Correiro Braziliense, in Portuguese, 16 November 1990, 5, translated in FBIS, LAT-91-006, 9 January 1991, 24. Another report, "Army Probing Drug Trafficking in Rondonia," O Estado de São Paulo, in Portuguese, 22 February 1993, 5, translated in FBIS, LAT-93-035, 24 February 1993, 22, also addresses this subject. In this report, the Army found the Federal Police organization so permeated with corruption associated with narcotics that they considered permanently appointing an Army colonel as commander of the police force.

[100]"Defense of the Calha Norte Project," O Estado de São Paulo, in Portuguese, 21 March 1987, 2, translated by JPRS, item # 10992.

project, the Army probably felt its goals should be in line with the Army objectives of non-involvement with a counter drug campaign. Thus, although the counterdrug campaign is no longer stipulated in the official goals of the project, it does still provide a rationale for the Army's involvement in the region.[101]

(3)   *Wildcat (illegal) Mining Operations.* The problems due to illegal mining operations have expanded slightly from 1985. The military estimates that of all economic activities currently being pursued in the Amazon region, 90 percent of them are illegal or irregular. These problems are now being compounded by Brazilian prospectors searching for gold in Venezuelan territory. These expanded operations by the Brazilian miners have resulted in increasing political tensions between the governments of Brazil and Venezuela.[102]

Both Brazil and Venezuela admitted to a need to better demarcate the border and solve the mining situation when, in 1991, a group of Venezuelan National Guardsmen evicted 25 FUNAI (the Brazilian Indian

---

[101]The military's continued concern with narcotics trafficking in the Amazon is highlighted in "High Command Studies Troop Reductions," O Estado São Paulo, in Portuguese, 2 March 1993, 7, translated in FBIS, LAT-93-042, 5 March 1993, 28.

[102]"Foreign Minister on Brazilian Prospectors," Caracas Venezolana de Televison Network (Caracas), in Spanish, 5 February 1993, translated in FBIS, LAT-93-025, 9 February 1993, 40.

Ministry) employees from the Brazilian town of Hamoxi.[103] Both countries

claimed sovereignty over the area, based on treaties ratified the previous

century. Brazil has since used the resources of the Calha Norte project to help

in the efforts to demarcate the borders in this region.

b. Budgetary Influences

The impact of military budgetary concerns behind the rationale

of the Calha Norte project is not as easy to assess as the geopolitical

connection. In order the prove the thesis of the expanding rationale, this

section will demonstrate that the Calha Norte project is used by the military to

justify its budget during the ongoing Brazilian economic crisis.

Unlike 1985, the military is no longer shielded against budgetary

cutbacks. They are now forced to justify their budgets along with all other

governmental agencies. In some cases, even when their expenditures are

justified they fail to receive monies as illustrated in the military pay debate.

The military pay debate probably best exemplifies the changes

in the Army's ability to "write its own check." In 1988, a military lobby effort

successfully resulted in the legislature authorizing a salary increase of 130

percent, making them the highest paid employees in the federal sector.[104] By

1991, military pay scales had fallen behind almost every other government

---

[103]"Venezuelan Military Incursions Reported," EFE (Madrid), in Spanish, 1 October 1991, translated in FBIS, LAT-91-192, 3 October 1991, 30.

[104]Zirker, 69.

sector pay scale. A move was made by the military to procure a 20 percent

pay raise that would have narrowed the margin of the pay scales but would

not have equated them. This move was unsuccessful, as Congress vetoed a

Presidential decree that would have implemented the raise. The problem

continued to plague the military in 1992 as they argued for a 301 percent

salary increase to compensate for prior losses.[105]

Not only did the military have problems procuring adequate

salaries but they were also unable to get funding for operational missions. In

1993, the military's budget as a share of total government expenditures had

decreased to only 2.6 percent of the federal budget, compared to 27 percent in

1983. This budget reduction resulted in the slowed progress of the Calha

Norte project, reduction in working hours for soldiers, and the degradation of

operational assets due to lack of maintenance funds.[106]

---

[105]"Armed Forces Protest Congress Salary Decision," EFE (Madrid), in Spanish, 3 July 1991, translated in FBIS, LAT-91-129, 5 July 1991, 26. See also "Military Wage Issue Continues to Simmer," O Globo, in Portuguese, 5 December 1990, 20, translated in FBIS, LAT-91-006, 9 January 1991, 26. This article describes the numerical disparity between military and other sector salaries. It cites the example of a police chief, retired from the federal police, that earns 476,000 cruzeiros compared a general with 45 years of service receives 260,000 cruzeiros. See also "Military Requests 301 Percent Salary Increase," O Globo, in Portuguese, 13 December 1992, 3, translated in FBIS, LAT-92-240, 14 December 1992, 33.

[106]"Senator Reports Further Cuts in Military Budget," Jornal do Brasil, in Portuguese, 5 December 1993, 3, translated in FBIS, LAT-92-243, 17 December 1992. See also "Army's Financial Difficulties Highlighted," O Estado São Paulo, in Portuguese, 11 August 1990, 5, translated in FBIS, LAT-90-158, 15 August 1990, 20. For more on operations effects of the budget crisis see "Army General Views Defense Industry Prospects," Tecnologia & Defesa, in Portuguese, May-June 1992, 5-8,

As the military budget shrinks, the Army has seemingly focused more emphasis on the Calha Norte project. Amidst the budgetary cuts that began in 1989, the Army proclaimed that the FT-90 program (the program which the Calha Norte project is under) would not be cut "even if other projects would have to be postponed."[107] The Army coordinated with the Superintendency for the Development of the Amazon (SADEN) and put together a book titled Calha Norte: Frontier of the Future. This book was an attempt to explain and justify the resource needs for the project. The book makes the argument that in order to accomplish the goals of the project, it should receive Cz$20 billion vice the Cz$11 billion it is allotted. It goes further to defend and detail specifically the costs associated with each aspect of the project--an action, which in previous times the military had not been required to perform.[108]

Other examples of the project being used to obtain operating funds include the Army presenting the project as the country's primary vehicle for achieving the "grandeza." Numerous Army statements have identified the

translated in FBIS, LAT-92-227, 24 November 1992, 31-34. See also "Impact of Military Budget Cuts Surveyed," Isto É/Senhor, in Portuguese, 22 April 1992, 26-29, translated in FBIS, LAT-92-107, 3 June 1992, 29-32.

[107]Translated and reported in FBIS, LAT-89-012a, 19 January 1989, 4.

[108]"Calha Norte Project To Get Cz$11 Billion," Jornal do Brasil, in Portuguese, 1 December·1988, 12, translated in FBIS, LAT-89-012a, 19 January 1989, 4. See also "Minister Defends Border Project, Requests Money," Jornal do Brasil, in Portuguese, 22 August 1991, 9, translated in FBIS, LAT-91-202-A, 18 October 1991, 2.

project with "national security and development" and of premier importance to Brazil. They are also quick to point out that although the project was initially started as an interministerial venture, the armed forces have been primarily responsible for its implementation. The lobbying efforts for the Calha Norte project have resulted in a nearly doubling of the project's budget and personnel.[109]

c. Institutional Legitimacy Influences

As illustrated in the previous section, the Army was able to successfully defend its institutional legitimacy following their removal from power in 1985. However, events in the subsequent years coupled with the revelation of harsh excesses of authoritarian rule, especially in the late 1960's and early 1970's, made the public question the legitimacy of the armed forces. The most prominent scandal was the "uniform" scandal. This incident involved the Army using questionable procurement procedures to obtain material such as clothing, linens, etc..[110] The public and media responded to this scandal with harsh criticism of the Army's actions. In addition to calls for external investigations into the matter, the press questioned the usefulness of

---

[109]U.S. Government Official, Washington, D.C., interviewed by author, 29 March 1993. See also "Calha Norte Project Given Higher Priority," Jornal do Brasil, in Portuguese, 2 November 1992, 4, translated in FBIS, LAT-92-243, 17 December 1992, 26.

[110]A more detailed account of this event can be found in "Army Approves Inflated Bids for Uniforms," O Globo, in Portuguese, 20 October 1991, reported and translated in FBIS, LAT-91-205, 23 October 1991, 16.

an armed forces organization at all. One report termed the actions of the military as the "Samba of the Nutty Soldier" and described in detail the military's failure to run a government (1964-1985) as well as their current inability to run a military.[111]

This loss of legitimacy has also affected the military's autonomy with respect to determining its operational policies and priorities. A March 1993 newspaper article related that military men have been excluded from major national decisions that relate to issues of national security and specifically the Amazon policy.[112]

In an attempt to restore this legitimacy, the Army has tried to project themselves as the nation builders, developers, and keepers of Brazilian national security. The current military leadership believes that continued national development is the solution to the Brazilian economic crisis. The Army has unrelentingly touted the Calha Norte project as the solution for unlocking the economic potential of the Amazon and therefore as of fundamental importance to Brazil. Additionally, they have cited the project as

---

[111]"Utility, Strength of the Armed Forces Debated," Veja, in Portuguese, 25 September 1991, translated in FBIS, LAT-91-204, 22 October 1991, 25. In this article the author cites the uniform scandal, the "threat" of internationalization of the Amazon, and other military embarrassments to make highlight the ineptness of the military. He continues by postulating that no military would be better than a military which bases operational plans on absurd scenarios and misuse of assets.

[112]"Military Club's Presidents Meet with President Franco," O Estado de São Paulo, in Portuguese, 9 March 1993, 5, translated by FBIS (Asuncion PA), in message dated R 101245Z MAR 93.

responsible for expanding the transportation infrastructure, strengthening trade cooperation with neighboring countries, and facilitating well-organized exploitation of water and mineral resources.[113]

The Army has displayed the same aggressiveness promoting its critical role within Calha Norte as it has trying to make national development synonymous with the project. Army press releases and official interviews constantly reference the expanded role that the military is playing within the project, given that other ministries have defaulted on their responsibilities to the project.[114] These reports and interviews have attempted to restore the public's confidence in the Army by presenting them in their historical role as nation builders. They downplay the military importance of the project, instead stressing how the project is directly affecting civilians of the region and the nation. Examples which they used to illustrate this national importance are: improvement of the infrastructure (international and domestic roads, and airstrips); provision of law and order to facilitate development; and most importantly, introduction of basic social services to the region.[115]

---

[113]"Minister Defends Border Project, Requests Money," Jornal do Brasil, in Portuguese, 22 August 1991, 9, translated in FBIS, LAT-91-202-A, 18 October 1991, 2. See also "Calha Norte Project Given Higher Priority," Jornal do Brasil, in Portuguese, 2 November 1992, 4, translated in FBIS, LAT-92-243, 17 December 1992, 26.

[114]"Calha Norte Program to be Decelerated," O Globo, in Portuguese, 7 June 1991, 7, translated in FBIS, LAT-91-133, 11 July 1991, 33.

[115]See Boletim Informativo, N°.26: XX Conferência Dos Exércitos Americanos, 24-26. See also "Calha Norte Project Given higher Priority," 26, "Implementation of Calha Norte Project Urged," 24 and "Minister Defends Border Project, Requests Money," 2.

C. SUMMARY AND DISCUSSION

Unquestionably, geopolitics had a large role to play in shaping the Calha Norte project in 1985. This conclusion is supported by the stated goals of the project, force locations, and the Army's historical involvement in the Amazon. What is just as apparent, following a review of the events, is that justification of a military budget and institutional legitimacy concerns did not play a significant role in implementing the project initially.

During the early and mid-1980's, the Brazilian Army retained a great deal of autonomy with regard to defining their own budget. In fact, one Army official felt that they gained even more autonomy over military budgetary matters by relinquishing power to the civilians in 1985.[116] The Armed Forces budget actually increased substantially following the transfer of power to the civilian regime in 1985.[117] The end result is that the military was able to get virtually any monies it wanted, with little or no justification for its expenditures. Thus, they had no reason to use the Calha Norte project as a justification for the military budget.

---

[116]Alfred Stepan, Rethinking Military Politics: Brazil and the Southern Cone, Princeton: Princeton University Press, 1988, 72.

[117]Military expenditures as a percentage of Central Government Expenditures were 3.2 percent in 1979 and dropped to 2.1 percent in 1985. Following the transfer of power to the civilians, this percentage was increased to 2.5 percent the very next year. Data taken from the World Military Expenditures and Arms Transfers, 1990 (WMEAT), U.S. Arms Control and Disarmament Agency, 55.

Similar to the budgetary issue, institutional legitimacy concerns were not included in the rationale behind the Army's push behind the <u>Calha Norte</u> project. Though the military had been discredited as political rulers, they still retained substantial legitimacy as a military institution. This fact was clearly illustrated behind the public acceptance of their historical role of external and internal defense of Brazilian society as well as the Armed Forces' successful efforts that prevented the consolidation of the three forces into a single ministry. Again, due to this solid foundation of legitimacy, the Army was not required to use the project as a means of supporting or reestablishing their legitimacy as a military institution.

However, by 1993 the dynamics of the military situation had changed from 1985. In 1993, as in 1985, geopolitics played a significant role in forming the rationale behind the <u>Calha Norte</u> project. Border insurgencies, drug trafficking, and illegal mining operations still provided a strong rationale to continue the project in 1993. However, contrary to the situation in 1985, geopolitics was not the only factor that comprised the rationale to implement <u>Calha Norte</u>. The political climate within Brazil had changed such that the Army no longer enjoyed its same status with regard to financial autonomy or mission integrity.

By 1993, the Brazilian economic crisis had become even more severe, and the military were forced to surrender some of the budgetary autonomy that they had exercised previously. The military, like all other federal agencies, were now required to justify their operational expenses in order to continue to receive funding. Complicating this matter was the uncovering of institutional scandals and other embarrassing events. These new revelations, combined with the previous 21 years of authoritarian rule, caused the Brazilian media and public to take a closer look at the military and their role and mission within society. The media began to question the need for an armed services, which served to hinder the military's request for additional funding. The combination of these events forced the military to not only justify their budget, but also their very existence as Brazil's guardians.

Calha Norte provided the Army with nearly the perfect solution to meet both of these new needs. It was a nation-building project that began as a joint venture between military and civilians whose goals were to benefit the civil society. The virtual exit of the civilian agencies from the project allowed the military to expand and fill the voids left by civilians. It now provided the military the perfect tool to justify both a budget (a military operation) and their new role and mission (developing the Amazon for civilian benefits).[118]

Thus, the rationale for the Calha Norte project has expanded since 1985 to include justification for the military's budget and relegitimation of the

---

[118]It should be noted that this is not really a new mission for the military, as they have historically been regarded as the nation builders and they have previously sought to develop the Amazon (see: History of Brazil in the Amazon). However, this represents the first plan offered by the military for a coordinated and supervised development of the Amazon instead of the previous laissez-faire plans.

institution. This expanded rationale has a noticeable physical effect on both the finances and resources assigned to the Calha Norte project by the Brazilian Army. In 1985, the commissioning year for Calha Norte, the project consisted of eight platoons stationed along strategic points on the borders. Command of each of these frontier posts was relegated to a junior officer. The initial plan called for the gradual increase in the number of platoons to eleven over the course of five years. Today, the project consists of nineteen platoons that are overseen by a brigade commander. Additionally, a brigadier general, the CMA, has been headquartered in Manaus to oversee all Amazon operations. Other moves intended to augment the military presence represented by the Calha Norte program include the transfer of two battalions and one brigade to the Amazon region.

The question still remains, can this expanded rationale explain the Army's increased presence in the Amazon Basin? If one were to look at the way which the Army has promoted the Calha Norte project and its self-defined new mission, the answer is yes. As illustrated above, the Army has been required to define its mission within the Brazilian community and fight for financial resources. It has used the Calha Norte extensively to accomplish both of these tasks.

With regard to defining their mission, the project has proven quite effective for the military. The collapse of communism and the warming of relations with Argentina left the Brazilian armed forces without an enemy to confront. The objectives of the Calha Norte project have served to establish a credible enemy in the form of drug traffickers, guerrillas, and other international forces that threaten to violate Brazilian sovereignty. Consequently, the project has provided the Army with a mission of defending the Amazon, which in turn has justified their expansion of the Calha Norte program.

In addition to providing protection of the region, the armed forces have ascribed to being the developers of the region. Aeronautics minister Brigadier General Octavio Moreiro Lima stated that "only the armed forces are in a position to initiate an orderly process of settling the border region."[119] The Army and the other military services are quick to point out that the project was initially started as a joint effort between various military and civilian ministries, with the Army's responsibility being to provide a military presence in the region. They also point out that the civilian ministries have forsaken the project due to the excessive hardships associated with the jungle environment and that the Army has stepped in to assume their obligations.[120] These additional responsibilities which they shouldered have served to highlight their

[119]"Defense of Calha Norte Project," O Estado Sao Paulo, in Portuguese, 21 March 1987, 2, translated in JPRS, item #10992.

[120]See "Strategic Affairs Secretary Mario Cesar Flores," O Estado Sao Paulo, in Portuguese, 13 October 1992, 5, translated in FBIS, LAT-92-216-S, 6 November 1992, 44. See also "Defense of Calha Norte Project" and "Calha Norte Project Given Higher Priority".

role as pioneers of Amazon regional development, but also the new civic

action role designed to benefit the local population.

III. IMPLICATIONS FOR CALHA NORTE PROJECT

Any military movement of significance has effects that can be felt throughout regional and international communities. These effects can be negative or positive depending on the specific situation. The Calha Norte project is no exception to this rule, as it has had both beneficial and detrimental impacts on each of these communities. This section will define and then evaluate the most serious of the implications associated with the Calha Norte project. The issues that will be evaluated are: 1) border conflicts; 2) the environment; and 3) narco-trafficking.

A.   POTENTIAL CONFLICTS

Border problems have long been a source of tension between Brazil and its neighbors, although they have not led to war this century. In his historical recount, "Geopolitics of the Amazon", Lewis A. Tambs stated that instabilities between Venezuela and Guyana, as well as the Peruvian Marcha para la Selva (March to the Forest) caused Brazil to intensify its presence in the Amazon region. As noted previously in Chapter II, nearly all land disputes between Latin countries have been resolved on the basis of *uti possidetis de facto*. While the political environment does not promote the expansionist policies of the past, the unstable national boundaries of the Amazon could cause countries to challenge each other's claims on forest resources.[121] Furthermore, the unmarked boundaries give rise to questions of illegal immigration and settlement that generate additional sources of friction between countries.

Calha Norte's buildup of military assets along the Amazon border has the potential to heighten the level of tensions between adjoining countries. This proved to be true when the project was initially revealed in 1986. Delegations from each of the border countries expressed to Itamaraty (Brazil's Ministry of Foreign Relations) apprehensions over Brazil's intentions in the region.[122] However, to assume that regional tensions will be heightened across the board would be inaccurate, as each of the Amazon border countries has a different relationships with Brazil. Therefore, in order to accurately assess how Calha Norte has influenced the potential for regional conflict, each of the border countries must be looked at individually.

---

[121]Robert J. Buschbacher explains that "national boundaries in the Amazon Basin region are sometimes rivers, sometimes watershed divides, but often there are no such natural delimitations. The frontier may be only an unmarked line running through the middle of the rain forest... River boundaries shift as new channels are cut and old ones are filled. Watershed divides change as new streams are discovered. Unmarked boundaries through rain forests are vague, and claims are easily challenged... Establishing a presence is an act of sovereignty and can serve as a precedent in any border disputes." See Robert J. Buschbacher, "Deforestation for Sovereignty Over Remote Frontiers," in Amazonian Rain Forests: Ecosystems Disturbance and Recovery, ed. Carl F. Jordan, New York: Springer-Verlag, 1987, 46.

[122]Elizabeth Allen, "Calha Norte: Military Development in Brazilian Amazônia", Development and Change, Vol. 23 (1992), 89.

Colombia

Calha Norte was specifically developed to combat border problems between Brazil and Colombia. As discussed in Chapter II, M-19 guerrillas had frequently crossed the border and harassed project platoons in the region. This led to Brazilian forces initiating an offensive into Colombian Amazon territory using land troops and fighter aircraft to combat the rebels. Tensions between the two countries increased when Brazilian forces detained two Colombian miners in international waters on the Taraira River during a search for the guerrillas. Additionally, Brazilian troops entered Colombian mines and opened fire killing three Colombian miners.[123]

These actions have apparently not created too much animosity between Colombia and Brazil, given that the topics were discussed during "routine bilateral talks."[124] In fact, these border incursions by the guerrillas have served to increase cooperation between Colombian troops and the Calha Norte platoons so as to address a common enemy. In March 1991, the CMA and commander of the Colombian Army's 4th Division met to devise joint plans to combat the guerrilla forces. The meeting also produced information exchanges, bilateral agreements on military cooperation, and other joint

---

[123]"Brazilian Border Operations Draw Attention," El Tiempo (Bogota), in Spanish, 26 March 1991, 6A, translated in FBIS, LAT-91-062, 1 April 1991, 37.

[124]Ibid, 37.

proposals between the two countries.[125] Indications of further strengthening

of ties came later in September 1991, when the two presidents met and signed

agreements concerning joint economic proposals, promotion of development,

and cooperation in the mutual legal assistance mechanisms. Probably the most

significant outcome of this meeting was the expressed joint satisfaction in

border operations involving both countries.[126]

Calha Norte has not adversely affected relations with Colombia, and in

fact has probably improved them. As long as the project's goals, with regards

to the border, remain complementary to Colombia's goals, there will be no

adverse effects on relations between the two countries.

Venezuela

Venezuela is the country where tensions with Brazil have increased the

most. The cause of this tension is directly related to one of the primary goals

of the Calha Norte project, settlement of the region. This goal of the project

has encouraged both the legal and wildcat miners (garimpeiros) to advance

---

[125]"Joint Antiterrorist Actions Planned With Colombia," Brasilia Radio Nacional da Amazonia Network, in Portuguese, 1000 GMT, 5 March 1991, translated in FBIS, LAT-91-044, 6 March 1991, 21. See also "Army Readies Anti-Guerrilla Plans with Brazil," Efe (Madrid), in Spanish, 0209 GMT, 11 March 1991, translated in FBIS, LAT-91-047, 11 March 1991, 40.

[126]"Agreements Signed, Joint Declarations," Brasilia Voz do Brasil Network, in Portuguese, 2200 GMT, 3 September 1991, translated in FBIS, LAT-91-171, 4 September 1991, 33.

deeper into the Amazon as they plunder the area for its resources. It has resulted in numerous illegal infringements on Venezuelan territories and destruction of Venezuelan land due to primitive mining techniques.[127] .

Venezuela has responded to these issues through both political and military channels. In the political arena, the Venezuelan government has attempted to work with the Brazilian government to find a solution to the problem, but has been unsuccessful thus far. These efforts were hampered when the candidate for the post of Brazilian ambassador to Venezuela commented that "Brazilian and Venezuelan military officers [were] interested in maintaining an atmosphere of confrontation."[128] such as these have only resulted in the deterioration of relations between the two countries, making the possibility of a quick diplomatic solution remote.

In addition to the war of words between Brazil and Venezuela, Venezuela has declared war on the miners. In April 1989, a group of 3,000 Brazilian miners was discovered in Venezuelan territory.[129] The mining camp had been established over one year and was equipped with a landing strip. After the miners had been returned to Brazil, Fernando César Mesquita, the Brazilian

---

[127]A description of the mining techniques and the subsequent damage it imposes on the environment is described in the environmental section of this chapter.

[128]"Foreign Minister on Brazilian Prospectors", Caracas Venezolana de Television Network, in Spanish, 2350 GMT, 5 February 1993. Translated in FBIS, LAT-93-025, 9 February 1993, 40.

[129]"Venezuelan Military to Expel 3,000 Miners" Efe (Madrid), in Spanish, 1556 GMT, 9 May 1989, translated in FBIS, LAT-89-089, 10 May 1989, 41.

Environmental Institute Chairman, attempted to land on the airstrip to meet with Venezuelan authorities concerning the situation. Venezuela's response was to chase Mesquita's helicopter back to Brazil, using Venezuelan fighter planes. In January of 1993, Venezuela arrested forty-six Brazilian miners they claimed were operating in Venezuelan territory.[130] The Brazilians claimed they were operating in Brazilian territory, intensifying the tension between the two nations and raising the issue of border demarcation.

The Calha Norte project could serve to ease tensions between Brazil and Venezuela if the Army uses the project to curb the excesses associated with both legal and illegal mining activities. In fact, as recently as February 1992, the Calha Norte platoons and Venezuelan troops performed joint operations to remove more than 10,000 gold prospectors who illegally occupied the area.[131] Continued successful operations and cooperation between the two militaries could serve to defuse the strained relationship between Brazil and Venezuela.

---

[130]"Itamaraty to Investigate Brazilian Held in Venezuela", Rio de Janeiro Rede Globo Television, in Portuguese, 1600 GMT, 11 February 1993, translated in FBIS, LAT-93-028, 12 February 1993, 17.

[131]"Operations Begin To Remove Brazilian Gold Prospectors", Caracas Venezolana de Television, in Spanish, 0000 GMT, 28 February 1993, translated in FBIS, LAT-93-038, 1 March 1993, 44.

Guyana

Border conflicts between Brazil and Guyana began in 1904. Brazil lost territory rich in mineral wealth to Guyana when, through arbitration, the king of Italy ruled in favor of Guyana. In 1969, the Guyanese Revolution overthrew the English colonial rulers, and chased the English citizens into Brazil. This resulted in a skirmish of gunfire between the two nations. The subsequent installation of a socialist government in Guyana, guided by Cuba, prompted Brazil to increase its presence along the border via the Calha Norte project. More recently, tensions flared slightly when Brazilian miners moved their operations into the Potari-Siparuni area of eastern Guyana.[132] However, the number of these miners was insignificant and Brazil was able to extract them from the region fairly quickly.

For the most part, Brazil and Guyana have cultivated a friendly political relationship since 1985. This relationship has yielded cooperation in several areas such as health programs, agriculture and livestock development, telecommunications and forest and mineral reserve programs. Thus, while Calha Norte increases Brazil's military resources along the border, it has not significantly added to the tensions between the two nations.

---

[132]"President Declares Brazilian Mining Illegal," Cana (Bridgetown), in English, 2116 GMT, 27 April 1990, reported in FBIS, LAT-90-083, 30 April 1990, 56.

Suriname

Like Guyana, the political stability of Suriname was one of the factors that initiated the Calha Norte project. Although the project was designed to keep unwanted socialist influences out of Brazil, it has not noticeably affected relations between the two countries. In June 1991, Brazil voiced the desire to reinforce political and economic ties between the two governments.[133] This news was favorably received in Suriname. In November 1992, the former dictator Desire Bouterse resigned as Armed Forces Commander prompting speculation of an attempted "military adventure" by Bouterse. Brazil was quick to reaffirm its commitment to the administration, demonstrating its positive relationship with the constitutional Surinamese government.[134]

Calha Norte has not threatened the Surinamese government and has therefore not adversely affected Suriname's relations with Brazil. Further, Suriname may view the project as a source of security. With an unstable political situation, and in light of the public support demonstrated by Brazil, Suriname could use the Brazilian military presence on the border to discourage political adventurism within the country. Thus, in this case, Suriname may actually encourage the growth of Calha Norte.

---

[133]"Collor Congratulates Suriname on Election Process," Paramaribo Radio Suriname International, in English, 1730 GMT, 10 June 1991, reported in FBIS, LAT-91-114, 13 June 1991, 32.

[134]"Government Supports Surinamese Government," Efe (Madrid), in Spanish, 2223 GMT, 26 November 1992, translated in FBIS, LAT-92-233, 3 December 1992, 23.

French Guiana

The French have not had any negative reactions to the military buildup by Brazil. Like Brazil, France views the problems of drug trafficking and gold smuggling as destabilizing. They have welcomed increased Brazilian efforts to eradicate the problems and have offered their cooperation. In March 1993, the two countries signed a treaty of mutual cooperation to combat gold and wood smuggling and narco-trafficking, using each country's custom agency as the focal point of collaboration.[135] If Calha Norte proves to be successful with regards to combatting these problems, the two countries could expand their treaty to encompass joint military operations as well.

Overall, none of the countries view the Calha Norte presence on their border as an invasion threat. It has increased tensions only in Venezuela, not because of the project itself, but because of the mining operations it has attracted to the Amazon. If Brazil does not rein in these renegade miners, history has shown their presence will continue to grow and spread into other countries. This will definitely result in strained relations between Brazil and Venezuela and, if left unchecked, could escalate out of control.

---

[135]"Agreement Signed With France on Drug, Gold Trafficking," Brasilia Voz do Brasil Network, in Portuguese, 2200 GMT, 19 March 1993, translated in FBIS, LAT-93-053, 22 March 1993, 27.

B. ENVIRONMENTAL IMPLICATIONS

Probably the most controversial topic with regards to the Calha Norte project has been the environmental concerns raised by domestic and international activists. The environmental impact of the project has been a source of friction between the military and environmental activists, and has hampered the growth of the project as originally envisaged.

The controversy centers around Calha Norte's goal to strategically develop the region for economic benefit. The Army's actions have provided physical and financial incentives, encouraging miners to migrate to the Amazon in search of gold and other mineral wealth. The Calha Norte project has provided miners with an infrastructure (airstrips, housing, etc.) that has been largely funded by the project's operations. These miners have been the source of environmentalist criticism. First, the mining operations have been responsible for numerous human rights violations against the indigenous population, jeopardizing their very survival. Secondly, most of the mining operations are small and not technically advanced (especially the illegal operations). The primitive mining techniques have resulted in significant pollution and destruction of local habitats.

One fourth of Brazil's 220,000 Indian population occupies about 20 percent of the land in the Calha Norte project. This has become the focal point of the environmental controversy surrounding the projects, given that "the areas surveyed as richer in mineral deposits are situated in indigenous [lands]...inhabited by the Yanomami Indians."[136] The potential wealth present in the Calha Norte region has been estimated at over US$134 billion, enough to repay almost all of Brazil's foreign debt.[137] Miners and other business enterprises, such as timber traders, have forcibly removed large numbers of the Indian population to gain access to these resources. Removal tactics have included abduction, terrorism, torture, and murder. Furthermore, the exposure of the Indians to these outsiders has resulted in an epidemic of malaria, gripe, colds, and influenza affecting more than 4,500 of the Indians.[138]

While the Calha Norte project was originally commissioned to establish a sensible Indian policy in the region, it has served only to confuse and worsen the plight of the Indians. The project certainly has the capability to remove the prospectors if it wanted to do so, as it proved in the Surucucu region in January of 1985. Recently, however, the project seems to favor the miners and timber merchants more than the Indians. In January 1990, the military succumbed to domestic and international pressure to remove the miners from Indian lands. The Army halted the operation the next day, citing the potential

---

[136]J.P. de Oliveiro Filho, "Segurança das frontieras e o novo indigenismo: formas e linhagem do Projeto Calha Norte", Antropologia e Indigenismo (1990), volume 1, 15-33.

[137]Bob Levin and Moyra Ashford, "The Last Frontier," Maclean's, 19 January 1987, 28.

[138]Linda Rabben, "Amazon Gold Rush: Brazil's Military Stakes its Claim," The Nation, 12 March 1990, vol. 250, n.10, 341.

for the miners' armed resistance. The decision to allow more than 40,000 garimpeiros to remain on Yanomami land was essentially a military decision. The Army's pro-miner position was highlighted by official statements made by the Army minister who said "Indians don't deserve to keep their lands because they're idle and lazy, don't work, and don't cultivate the soil."[139]

The Army's inaction regarding protection of Indian lands has resulted in a population explosion of miners, exploding from the original 60 armed prospectors of the Surucucu region to an estimated 50,000 prospectors present in the region today.[140] This increase in population has intensified violence against the Indians, reducing some tribes to less than 10 members.[141] The military and government's failure to address this aspect of the Calha Norte project has allowed this violence to escalate with impunity. One author has suggested that the Army's indifference is due to soldiers participating in goldmining activities.[142] If the current situation continues, the very existence of the Indian population will be threatened.

---

[139]Rabben, 341.

[140]Allen, 91. Official estimates of the garimpeiro population place the number of miners between 30,000-35,000. However, sources involved in the Amazon region have stated that the number could be as high as 100,000.

[141]"Brazil: Indigenous People Under Siege by Land Grabbers," EcoNet, Inter Press Service (1993), 0546:17 GMT, 9 February 1993.

[142]Rabben, 341.

In addition to the human rights issues, the mining operations have also increased the amount of environmental pollution in the Amazon. Goldmining operations extract the gold deposits using cheap, but highly destructive, removal methods. Typically, the removal takes place in the riverbeds. Miners use high pressure water pumps to erode river banks, producing a muddy effluent that potentially contains gold. This phase of the process ruins the natural habitats of local species, as well as destroying the vegetation. The miners then channel the muddy runoff into troughs, adding large quantities of toxic mercury compounds to separate the gold from the mud. Most of this mercury cannot be recovered, escaping into the river where it poisons the food chain.[143]

These destructive mining practices, if left unchecked, could endanger the very survival of the Amazon. Ecologist David Quammen describes the Amazon as a very sensitive ecosystem in which every aspect of the system is interdependent on the others for its survival.[144] Thus the destruction of a tree or of the surrounding humus would result in the death of the surrounding area.

Consequently, if the Calha Norte project continues to ignore the actions of miners and timber merchants, the survival of the Amazon and its

---

[143]Andres L. Pacheco, Staff Engineer, Aspen Technology, Inc., phone interview by author, 14 May 1993.

[144]Quammen, 45.

inhabitants is questionable. Past performance would indicate that the Army does not see a problem in the area. Retired General Antenor Santa Cruz, former head of the CMA and now retired, has publicly stated that "all the tropical forest remains intact," rejecting theories that the Amazon was adversely affected by these development influences. He went further, saying that people should not concern themselves with the Indians as "no one is better off" in Brazil.[145]   Current Brazilian policies do not support a stronger stand on the part of the Calha Norte project with respect to the environment. The policies in place favor big mining corporations and programs that will develop the region into an economically productive sector of Brazil.[146] The future of the Amazon environment, therefore, appears to be one of continual decline.

[145]"General Defends 'Calha Norte' Project," Zero Hora (Porto Allegre), in Portuguese, 13 June 1992, translated and reported in USDAO document Brazil #IIR 6 809 0573 92. Interestingly, the General based his opinion of the welfare of the Indians based on their land holdings. He stated that Indian reserves totalled 900,000 km^2, which averages 400 hectares per Indian. He failed to note that specific tracts of land change on almost a monthly basis due to mining permits granted by the government. Additionally, he made no mention of the brutality that is used to uproot the Indians from their land when it is expropriated.

[146]For a more in depth description of the environmental policies of Brazil see Bruce Allen, "Indian Lands, Environmental Policy and Military Geopolitics in the Development of the Brazilian Amazon: The Case of the Yanomami," Development and Change (1992), vol. 23, 35-70.

C.   COUNTERDRUG IMPLICATIONS

One of Calha Norte's original goals was to combat narco-trafficking in the Amazon region. And, though it is not specifically delineated in the most current mission statement, counterdrug operations remain a high priority for project coordinators. According to U.S. government officials, however, the project has made little impact on drug-trafficking within the border regions.[147] The failure of the program, with regards to this goal, is attributed to a lack of sufficient presence in the region. Only 19 platoons exist, manned by approximately 70 soldiers each. Of these soldiers only 30 are trained for combat, the rest providing administrative and supply support for the installation. This translates to about 570 soldiers responsible for 1,200,000 km^2, or 2100 km^2 per soldier. Small wonder, then that the project has had little effect on the drug problem.

In response to this situation, the Amazon Command has proposed the installation of a radar system, which would monitor air space over the Amazon for small aircraft. The project would identify potential drug-smuggling aircraft and then direct troops to interdict and apprehend the perpetrators.[148] This program would enhance current efforts, as border

[147]U.S. Government Official, Office of the Secretary of Defense, interview by author, Washington, DC, 27 March 1993.

[148]For an in-depth description of this system see "Amazon Surveillance System," pamphlet published by the Brazilian Air Force, distributed to the United States Department of Defense, 1992.

platoons now lack any dedicated air support that would enable them to respond to crisis areas. However, similar systems employed by the U.S. in the fight against drugs have been relatively unsuccessful. It is unlikely then, that the new Brazilian initiative will prove successful, given that the program is responsible for more area and employs fewer people in the operation.

Another counterdrug operation that used Calha Norte forces was the dynamiting of airstrips used by drug traffickers in the state of Roraima.[149] This operation was relatively unsuccessful given that the airstrips were repaired within one week of their destruction.[150]

Currently Calha Norte forces do not have the ability to affect the drug-trafficking operations that plague the area. Even with the proposed increase in materiel, the project still lacks the resources to effectively combat the problem. To provide an effective campaign against drug-trafficking, Brazil must dedicate more assets to the Amazon region. If more assets are not assigned for the

---

[149]"Destruction of Clandestine Airstrips to Begin," Brasilia Radio Nacional da Amazonia Network, in Portuguese, 1000 GMT, 2 May 1990, translated in FBIS, LAT-90-086, 3 May 1990, 32. See also "Blasting of Clandestine Landing Strips Continues," Brasilia Domestic Service, in Portuguese, 2200 GMT, 14 May 1990, translated in FBIS, LAT-90-094, 15 May 1990, 26.

[150]U.S. Government Official, Office of Secretary of Defense, interview by author, Washington, DC, 29 March 1993.

counter-drug campaign, no significant progress will be realized in this

fight.[151]

D.   U.S. POLICY OPTIONS

It is unrealistic to believe the United States could unilaterally influence

the Calha Norte project via U.S. policy measures. However, given that U.S.

security interests (primarily counterdrug) are affected by Calha Norte, it is not

unreasonable for the U.S. to formulate a policy that addresses the program.

Such a U.S. policy could take the form of one of four options: 1) opposition; 2)

benign neglect; 3) indirect support; and 4) direct support. These policy options

are listed in order of magnitude of U.S. support for the project, from lowest to

highest, and are described below.

Opposition

The Catholic Church, human rights, and environmental organizations

have lobbied to have the Calha Norte project cease operations. These efforts

stem from allegations that the military has abandoned their protective mission

of the Indians in support of the military's regional development mission. The

groups argue that the military has given little consideration to designated

---

[151]The author is heavily indebted to Roy Kitchener for his views and research on the Brazilian Military and their role in counter-drug activities. See "The Brazilian Military: Its Role in Counter-drug Activities," Master's Thesis, Naval Postgraduate School, June 1992.

Indian lands when planning developmental projects that in turn have destroyed much of the Indians' habitat. They additionally argue that the military has increasingly sided with mining interests when resolving land dispute issues. This in turn has further endangered the survival of the Indians. The critics use these points to advocate curtailing the Calha Norte project instead of enlarging it. Such arguments suggest that the United States should adopt a policy of opposition to Calha Norte.

The environmentalists' accusations are only half correct. While the military is not entirely innocent, neither are they directly responsible. The garimpeiros and their operations are mainly responsible for these atrocities while the military is only guilty of observing and doing nothing to stop it. Requiring the military to scale down or abandon Calha Norte will do nothing to improve the situation in the Amazon with regards to these issues as the miners will still remain.

This policy option is not recommended because it would not solve the problems in the Amazon and it would most likely result in the United States losing future opportunities to affect Brazilian policy. As presented above, the Calha Norte project, and its associated goals, have become of great significance to the Brazilian military with regard to defining their role and mission. Consequently, any attempt to oppose this project would certainly be viewed as interventionist, and therefore would be hotly contested by the military and civilians alike. The nationalistic feelings incited by such a move would effectively remove the United States from any type of bargaining leverage that they may enjoy today with Brazil.

This paper does not suggest, nor intend to imply, that relations with Brazil are critical to the survival of the United States or the future success of its policies. However, the Latin American region is slowly emerging as a force to be reckoned with both economically and militarily.[152] Alienation of Brazil at this stage of U.S.-Brazilian relations could present unsurmountable obstacles towards improving relations in the future. This disaffection would directly curtail the prospects of an expanded U.S. regional role for later negotiations.

Benign Neglect

The "benign neglect" option would have the U.S. essentially ignore Brazilian moves in the Amazon. This option assumes that, no matter what Brazil chooses with regard to the Calha Norte project, it will not produce any outcomes that would drastically change the Amazonian situation with respect to U.S. objectives. Consequently, the U.S. would not have to expend

---

[152]Both Chile and Argentina have demonstrated strong, sound economic policies that have translated into booming producer and consumer economies. Other countries are slowly incorporating these two models into their own economies to recreate the success stories. Militarily, Brazil and Argentina have strong weapons industries and have demonstrated the ability to pursue nuclear weapons. Although a nuclear weapons free zone has been informally established in Latin America (Treaty of Tlatelolco) Brazil's intentions to formally ratify the treaty are suspect. Recently, Brazil has actively pursued development of a nuclear-powered submarine and other nuclear power technology that could be converted easily to nuclear weapons.

outcomes that would drastically change the Amazonian situation with respect to U.S. objectives. Consequently, the U.S. would not have to expend diplomatic and fiscal resources in an attempt to influence Brazil. Given the recent apprehension between Brazilian and U.S. diplomats, the neglect option also has the advantage of shielding the U.S. from Latin American accusations of "interventionism," as this policy advocates letting each country pursue its objectives unhindered.

While the neglect policy would produce the least amount of tension between the two countries, it would not be very effective with regards to achieving U.S. objectives. Even if Brazil expands the Calha Norte project to support counterdrug objectives, the country does not possess the resources to institute an effective campaign against the narco-traffickers. Therefore, U.S. resources and expertise could assist the Brazilians in mounting this campaign. Under this option the U.S. is also not likely to realize its environmental objectives. This is due to the fact that Brazil's environmental policies are unlikely to change without external pressures (see above: Environmental Impact of Calha Norte).

Indirect Support

Since the early 1980's relations between the United States and Brazil have deteriorated because Brazil thinks the United States has blocked its path to "first world" status. Brazil views itself as engaged in a "patron-client" relationship with the United States and characterizes that relationship as the obstacle that prevents its progress towards modernization. In the past, Brazilian nationalism has hampered U.S. attempts at diplomacy within the region. The current situation does not look much brighter for U.S. policies vis-a-vis Brazil.

International diplomacy might provide a solution to overcome this barrier and allow a functional policy to evolve in Brazil. This option would involve the United States' coordination of Brazilian policies through multilateral rather than bilateral channels. The multilateral relationship could be achieved through organizations such as the Organization of American States (OAS) or the United Nations. The success of such a relationship with Brazil has been proved in the past as illustrated in regards to illegal mining operations in the Amazon. Brazil's original attempts to expel the renegade miners from the Amazon were initiated only after intense pressure by governmental and nongovernmental actors from the international arena. The OAS option is particularly attractive given that the policy prescriptions would be coming from Brazil's Latin American peers rather than the United States or Europe.

This policy option does not suggest that all direct relations between the U.S. and Brazil be severed in favor of multilateral relations. On the contrary, relations such as military and trade should remain bilateral to better enhance regard for the United States within Brazil. When the United States tries to shape or affect Brazilian domestic policy, however, the international diplomacy option would have the best chance of success.

Direct Support

Direct diplomacy would require the United States to work directly with Brazil in promulgating U.S. policy. As mentioned above, this option runs a great risk of being viewed by Brazil as another attempt by the U.S. to intervene in Brazilian domestic affairs. As such, Brazil would disregard any goals or objectives put forth by the U.S. under this type of policy. The "direct" option would fuel Brazilian nationalism and defeat any hope for a successful U.S. policy vis-a-vis Brazil. Under the current political conditions within Brazil, the U.S. should refrain from adopting this type of policy.

Recommendations

Previously, a conflict with Argentina dominated Brazilian security concerns. However, given that Brazilian-Argentine relations have drastically improved, this threat seems to have subsided. Replacing this threat has been the narco-trafficking trade presently growing in the Brazilian Amazon. For years the United States has attempted to convince the Brazilian military to adopt a counterdrug mission. The Brazilian military has refused on the grounds that they are not prepared for the mission. They cite lack of funds and personnel training as reasons for avoiding the task. More importantly, though, Brazil sees U.S. demands as an act of interventionism that affronts Brazilian sovereignty. The present Brazilian counterdrug mission, which is currently headed by the Federal Police (PF), has been ineffective, lacking sufficient manning to adequately patrol the country's borders and jungle region. The PF is responsible for providing for providing counter-narcotics coverage for all of Brazil, yet is only comprised of 6,000 personnel. The PF Director General, Amauri Gaudino, stated that the PF should have a minimum of 25,000 members to perform their function adequately.[153]

Brazil understands the threat that narcotics imposes, but economic reality dictates that resources are not available to expand the PF as Gaudino recommends. However, given the regional situation, the Calha Norte project, which also currently lacks both personnel and resources to mount a counterdrug offensive, could provide a solution to Brazil's narcotics problems. Since Argentina no longer poses a valid threat to Brazil, the military could expand the Calha Norte project by transfering Southern Command assets to the CMA. This could be done with little to no added cost to the government. These additional resources would enhance Calha Norte's counterdrug abilities, and result in a relatively small impact on the military's operating budget. A U.S. policy in favor of such an initiative would not be viewed as interventionist as it would be complementary to Brazilian conceived goals.

---

[153]"Drug Trafficking Rise Blamed on Police Crisis," Efe (Madrid), in Spanish, 0149 GMT, 19 February 1993, translated in FBIS, LAT-93-034, 23 February 1993, 22.

This effort would make a Brazilian counterdrug mission more palatable and more effective.

Given these arguments, it is this author's opinion that the United States should support an expansion of the Calha Norte project through a policy of indirect support. This will allow the necessary resources and technologies to be made available to Brazil such that the project may become an effective counterdrug vehicle while avoiding the potential frictions of a direct support policy.

While this thesis recommends a policy supporting an augmentation of the Calha Norte project, it does not favor a policy of unrestricted expansion. An increased Brazilian Army presence in the Amazon by itself will do nothing to change the situation either. Brazil's past history suggests that the increased Brazilian presence would simply result in more soldiers standing idly by, observing the abuse of the indigenous population. In order to protect international environmental interests in the Amazon, the United States must couple support for the Calha Norte project with demands for stronger Indian policies and mining regulations from the Brazilian government.

Critics further worry that the expansion of Calha Norte could result in a state within a state, increasing the political leverage of the military within society. The business interests and population of the Amazon would owe their livelihood and their allegiance to the military for its development of the region. While it remains a possibility, the likelihood of Calha Norte encouraging an increased political role for the military is remote. This was illustrated during the 1992 crisis over the Fernando Collor de Mello administration, where the military took great pains to distance itself from a sticky political situation. Public statements by active and retired military officials indicated that they wanted this matter to be handled solely by the civilian government. The military clearly indicated that they desired to avoid the same politicized role in the government that they enjoyed eight years ago during the military administration. Thus, an expansion of the <u>Calha Norte</u> program does not seem to endanger democracy and civilian rule at this juncture. However, to further insure that the civilian institutions do not suffer from an expanded <u>Calha Norte</u> project, all U.S. diplomatic action, no matter which option is employed, should be made through Itamaraty. By empowering the civilian institutions with diplomatic negotiations, the U.S. will help to secure civilian control over the military institution.

IV. CONCLUSION

The introduction raised a number of important issues, such as: (1) Brazil's rationale for occupation of the Amazon; (2) security implications of the <u>Calha Norte</u> project with regards to regional and international interests; and (3) policy options for the United States vis-a-vis Brazil and the <u>Calha Norte</u> project. This section will summarize the findings of the paper and provide recommendations for further research.

A. SUMMARY OF FINDINGS

In 1985, the <u>Calha Norte</u> project was authorized by the Brazilian government to achieve geopolitical goals and secure the Amazon. However, since 1985, the military's rationale for the <u>Calha Norte</u> project has expanded. The project still provides a vehicle for the Army to achieve the geopolitical goals of economically harnessing the Amazon and establishing a military and security presence in the region. In addition, changing economic and political situations within Brazil have encouraged the military to use the project for more than geopolitical purposes. The shrinking military budget and changing international threats have caused the military leadership to justify itself in areas where it had previously enjoyed autonomy. This has led to a redefinition of the <u>Calha Norte</u> project as more than an operation to achieve geopolitical ends for the country, but also as one that

100

satisfies the country's need for national development. By portraying the project as one of necessary civic action, the military is able to rationalize and defend its budget before the Brazilian general public. Further, the project serves to substitute the protection and development of the Brazilian Amazon as the Army's mission for that of defender against the disappearing threats of Soviet communism and Argentine hostilities. Consequently, as the military's rationale for the project has grown, so to have the resources that they have invested in the project.

The growth of the Calha Norte project has had the potential to affect both regional and international security interests. Regionally, the military buildup of Calha Norte has not had the anticipated affect of heightening local tensions. In fact, with the exception of Venezuela, Calha Norte has strengthened bilateral relations as it pursues goals common to Brazil's neighbors. The case of Venezuela stands out because of the excessive illegal mining activity occurring on the border regions between the two countries. Although the project is not directly responsible for the presence of the miners, the infrastructure introduced to the region by Calha Norte has served to encourage mining operations in the Amazon. This problem must be seriously and carefully addressed by Brazil, because ignoring the problem will only allow the miners to extend their operations into other countries. This will almost certainly reproduce the tensions of the Venezuelan-Brazilian relationship within other countries of the Amazon region.

Lastly, the United States should take advantage of the opportunity that the Calha Norte project presents to advance U.S. goals within the region. The project represents the Brazilian Army's first real attempt to mount a counterdrug campaign in the Amazon region. Although critics postulate that the military project threatens the environment and indigenous populations, Calha Norte has had only a small effect on these two issues. The real danger to the environment is posed by the mining operations present in the Amazon and the official Brazilian mining policies under which they operate. Thus, even if the Army were to withdraw from the region, this action would not necessarily cause the miners to leave as well. The end result would be the continued imperilment of the Amazon's resources and population.

Ironically, one of Calha Norte's objectives is to curtail the harmful wildcat mining operations and secure the safety of the Amazon's indigenous population. For the most part, forces have been ineffectual in achieving these objectives. However, the Army has proven its capability to fulfill these objectives when motivated to do so. In the past, this motivation has taken the form of domestic and international pressure exerted by government and environmental organizations. A removal or reduction of the Army's presence in the region would result in the loss of this tool to combat the current environmental destruction.

The United States must be careful how it encourages Brazil, as Brazil is very sensitive about its sovereignty in relation to the Amazon. If Brazil senses that the

U.S.-Brazil relationship is to be one of a "patron-client", Brazil will be less likely to respond to U.S. overtures.

The United States has three policy options that it could use to encourage the Calha Norte project: benign neglect, indirect support, and direct support. The benign neglect option assumes that Brazil will expand the project on its own without encouragement, and therefore advocates a laissez-faire policy on the part of the United States. The indirect support option advocates that the U.S. encourage the Calha Norte using international organizations such as the OAS. Finally, the direct support option recommends the United States work directly with Brazil to encourage the project.

The thesis recommends that the United States adopt the indirect support policy option and work through international organizations. This policy option would have a greater chance of success as it provides encouragement for the project while avoiding being criticized for interventionism. To support strengthening of democratic institutions, these organizations for U.S. policy should funnel all contacts made in Brazil through Itamaraty, a civilian institution.

B. AREAS FOR FUTURE RESEARCH

This paper has illustrated an expanding rationale for the Calha Norte program. The expanded rationale has coincided with an expanded Army presence in the Amazon, raising issues that require further research. First, there is a need to determine how the Calha Norte project can best focus its resources to combat narco-trafficking. Even with the expanded resources planned for the project combined with those recommended by this paper, the Army is not set up to combat narco-trafficking. Additional training and organization is required to accomplish this task.

Second, an expanded <u>Calha Norte</u> project has the potential to work to protect the environment if it is supported by sound policy in Brasília. Further research is needed to develop policies that can work to complement the military presence in the Amazon to achieve environmental goals.

Third, the project claims to promote the development of the region. Additional research should focus on the actual operation of the frontier posts, and whether or not this model of development will be successful for the Amazon region.

Lastly, civilian involvement within <u>Calha Norte</u> has been virtually abandoned. Further research should be performed to determine whether and where civilian responsibilities should be reinstated in the project.

www.ingramcontent.com/pod-product-compliance
Lightning Source LLC
Chambersburg PA
CBHW080310290526
45790CB00005B/1982